DATE DUE

DEMCO 38-296

THE IMMIGRANT EXPERIENCE IN AMERICAN FICTION
An Annotated Bibliography

by
Roberta Simone

The Scarecrow Press, Inc.
Lanham, Md., & London

ca

by Scarecrow Press, Inc.
4720 Boston Way, Lanham, Maryland 20706

4 Pleydell Gardens, Folkestone
Kent CT20 2DN, England

British Cataloging in Publication Information Available

Library of Congress Cataloging-in-Publication Data

Simone, Roberta.
The immigrant experience in American fiction : an
annotated bibliography / by Roberta Simone.
p.   cm.
Includes indexes.
1. American Fiction—Bibliography.   2. Emigration and
immigration in literature—Bibliography.   3. Immigrants in
literature—Bibliography.   I. Title.
Z1231.F4S56   1995   [PS374.I48]   016.813008—dc20   94–37400

ISBN 0–8108–2962–2 (cloth : alk. paper)

Printed in the United States of America

 The paper used in this publication meets the minimum requirements of
American National Standard for Information Sciences—Permanence
of Paper for Printed Library Materials, ANSI Z39.48–1984.

To the memory of Iole Gianneschi Simone, Giovanni Battista Simone, and John Charles Simone; and to the future of Tony and Skye Chamberlain, Mallika, Meru, Tony, and Allegra Simone.

CONTENTS

FOREWORD

As post-structuralist theory undermines the notions of transcendence and universality typically ascribed to the traditional canon, literary revisionists seek to correct the distorted record of American letters that has long prevailed. These scholars, in their efforts to present an account of literary production in the United States that is more comprehensive and thus more representative than the limited and subjective Anglo-American paradigm, are directing their attention to the deliberately ignored or casually overlooked stories of marginalized Americans. Professor Simone's *The Immigrant Experience in American Fiction* makes an important contribution to this movement to reconstruct American literary history.

Minority studies have burgeoned since the turbulent 1960s. Spurred by the gains of the civil rights movement, those who have been barred from full participation in the literary tradition—women, homosexuals, ethnic Americans—eagerly assert their "right to be represented in the picture America draws of itself."[1] The field of immigrant literature, a branch of ethnic writing distinguished by the choice to relocate to the United States, which is at the root of these stories about the perils and pleasures of becoming American, follows roughly the same development into the viable, scholarly endeavors which African-American and feminist literary studies took. Traceable in the works annotated in this reference guide are similar stages of evolution: stereotypical portrayals of immigrants in mainstream writing; fiction about the immigrant experience written by first-generation Americans and their descendants; and the formation of conceptual grounds for the critical inquiry into that body of writing.

As is characteristic of much post-modern thought, there is little consensus about what constitutes "ethnic" or "immigrant" literature. Enikö Molnár Basa stipulates that literature can be considered

---

[1] Jane Tompkins, *Sensational Designs: The Cultural Work of American Fiction, 1790-1866* (New York: Oxford University Press, 1985) 163-165. Tompkins is referring to feminist critics of female sentimental novelists. Her words apply, however, to all American minorities.

"Hungarian-American," for example, only if it is written by members of that ethnic group.[2] Rose Basile Green further restricts that criterion when defining Italian-American literature, by contending that the writers not only must be of Italian ancestry, but must also consistently project "values that are uniquely Italian."[3] Juan Bruce-Novoa, discussing the tension among Chicano writers as they try to define the parameters of their literature, explains that the term and category of "Chicanesque" is meant to designate and recognize literature about Chicanos that is written by non-Chicanos.[4] Dorothy Burton Skårdal looks to readership to determine whether or not one is in fact an ethnic writer. Because Carl Sandburg draws a following from across the spectrum of the American population, she contends that this second-generation Swedish-American is not an ethnic writer.[5] But because *The Immigrant Experience* includes fiction written by first-generation Americans and their descendants, as well as by novelists who did not belong to the ethnic group about which they wrote, the bibliography's scope is not constrained by narrow or contradictory definitions of the genre.

In those books written by well-known, often majority-group authors who are not part of the group that is their literary subject, it is often possible to infer their superficial understanding of or their negative attitudes toward the immigrants they describe. For instance, in *The Jungle* (1905), most of Upton Sinclair's hapless Lithuanian immigrants are subdued by the ordeal of relocation and by brutalizing work in Chicago's meatpacking industry. Sinclair was more interested in exposing capitalist exploitation than in presenting the immigrant culture. Similarly, Nelson Algren used Polish immigrants as the vehicle for his own naturalist message. Chicago's Poletown in *The Neon Wilderness* (1947) is a depraved place; its pathetic inhabitants are inexorably doomed. The Bohemian immigrants of Willa Cather's *My Antonia* (1918), at least as the protagonist Jim Burden sees them, cover a range of stereotypes: Mr. Shimerda, Antonia's romantic father, commits suicide because he cannot adjust to his harsh new life in

---

[2]"Hungarian-American Literature," *Ethnic Perspectives in American Literature: Selected Essays on the European Contribution*, eds. Robert Di Pietro and Edward Ifkovic (New York: MLA, 1983) 90.

[3]"Italian-American Literature," *Ethnic Perspectives* 111.

[4]"Canonical and Noncanonical Texts," *Redefining American Literary History*, eds. A. LaVonne Brown Ruoff and Jerry W. Ward, Jr. (New York: MLA, 1990) 205.

[5]*The Divided Heart: Scandinavian Immigrant Experience through Literary Sources.* (Lincoln: University of Nebraska Press, 1974) 47-48.

Nebraska; Krajiek, Shimerda's conniving countryman, cheats his fellow immigrants for his own gain; Antonia is an earthmother, who thrives through her seventeen pregnancies out on the untamed Western plains.

Correspondingly, several citations in the bibliography give evidence that immigrants and their descendants were capable of their own stereotyping, possibly to pander to public expectations and thus to guarantee a readership. Consider, for example, *Chinatown Family* (1948) by Lin Yu Tang, in which the Fongs are the model minority, hardworking and making no demands on the white society, happy to accept the United States on its own terms—a stereotype that still seems to persist about Chinese immigrants. At the same time, Monfoon Leong's more realistic *Number One Son* was consistently rejected for publication because it would not appeal to the mainstream. Better known is Mario Puzo's *The Godfather* (1969). This sensational story of the Mafia underworld found the readership which eluded *The Fortunate Pilgrim* (1964), Puzo's earlier novel about a typical immigrant family struggling to survive with dignity and eventually escaping the straitened conditions of New York's Little Italy.

For the most part, *The Immigrant Experience* exemplifies the middle stage of ethnic literary historiography, its primary objective being to recover and collect fiction written by immigrants or their descendants about the tolls and rewards of becoming American. The earliest citations therein are Irish novels, Father Hugh Quigley's *The Cross and the Shamrock* (1853), describing the exploitation of Irish laborers and Yankee persecution of their Catholicism, and Mary Anne Sadlier's *Confessions of an Apostate* (1864), exploring the tragic consequences of trying to mask nationality. Both books caution against assimilation of a Caucasian, English-speaking group that could easily blend into the American mainstream. The most recent citations are from the 1990s, books primarily about Central and South Americans, Cubans, and Asians. Together, all the fictional works which are listed in this bibliography, published between the mid-nineteenth and late-twentieth centuries, reveal shifting trends in the production and reception of immigrant literature, as well as in actual patterns of immigration.

Most fiction set during the largest stage of the great migration, the Mediterranean-Slavic wave dating from 1890 to 1914, was written not by immigrants themselves but by their children or grandchildren. This pattern of authorship is due, in part, to the circumstances that surrounded removal and relocation. Largely non-Protestant or non-Christian, these "new" immigrants (as opposed to "old" immigrants, who came predominantly from northern and western Europe on and off between 1815 and 1890) were mainly peasants, artisans, and shopkeepers driven from their homelands by political, religious, and economic oppression. As a result, many who immigrated at the turn of the last century were consumed by the tasks of providing for their families and trying to save money to bring over more family members or to return home to buy land. They often lacked both the time and the know-how to create written literature; some were literate neither in English nor their native language. Quite understandably then, it usually took a generation or two before an ethnic-American family produced a writer. There are significant exceptions, however. Abraham Cahan, for example, learned English quickly and published such novels as *Yekl*, 1896, and *The Rise of David Levinsky*, 1917. Many immigrant intellectuals published in their native language, as did Ole Rölvaag, though he helped translate his work from Norwegian into English.[6] Furthermore, there was little support for non-mainstream publishing during a period of institutionalized xenophobia and nativism, exemplified by the Chinese Exclusion Act of 1882 or the Know-Nothing Party of the mid- to late-nineteenth century, which elected congressmen and governors and backed a presidential candidate on an anti-Catholic platform. Books by ethnic writers that found publishers were often panned, regarded as flawed if they did not conform to the accepted standards of aesthetics and often deemed to be sociology rather than literature.

Through his influential thesis, "what the son wishes to forget, the grandson wishes to remember,"[7] Marcus Hansen attempted to explain what he saw as the reticence and shame of many second-generation Americans about their ethnic descent and the reversal in attitude as the third generation eagerly rediscovered their immigrant origins. Indeed, much immigrant fiction tells the story of families divided, as children resist and reject the old-world ways of their parents and are drawn instead into American culture. Yet the very fact that a good deal of immigrant fiction is written by second-generation Americans seems to disprove Hansen's claim. (Hansen himself is a "son," a second-generation Scandinavian-American whose contributions to immigrant

---

[6] For additional writers who composed and published in their native tongue, see Wolodymyr Zyla and Wendell Aycock, eds., *Ethnic Literature Since 1776: The Many Voices of America*, 2 vols. (Lubbock: Texas Tech University, 1978) or Di Pietro and Ifkovic's *Ethnic Perspectives*.

[7] Marcus Lee Hansen, "The Third Generation in America," *Commentary* 14 (1952): 494.

studies prove that he did not "forget" his roots.) Certainly, protagonists often renounce the old-world customs and values of their parents, but equally as often they come to reconcile themselves to their dual identity. As a case in point, some of the fiction collected in Oscar Handlin's *Children of the Uprooted* (1966) was written by authors who describe their lives in ethnic enclaves with immigrant parents. Jerre Mangione's *Mount Allegro* (1943) excerpted in it is typical of protagonists' growing interest in their foreign ancestry; for instance, Gerlando Amoroso, Mangione's main character, travels to Sicily to experience the world his parents left behind. Hansen's generational paradigm, as well as his sexism (as seen in his focus only on male descendants),[8] are further challenged by publishing trends from the mid-twentieth century and beyond.

Interest in ethnicity grew stronger in the aftermath of the 1960s, creating an atmosphere that was favorable to publishing multicultural literature. In addition, immigrants entering the United States during the 1940s and later differed from those who came at the beginning of the century in such matters as reasons for leaving home and the social and economic conditions left behind. Many recent immigrants from Eastern Europe and Southeast Asia were displaced by war; a greater number than earlier immigrants found easier access to universities. Heightened interest in America's ethnic pluralism, as well as the higher levels of education some of the more recent immigrants were able to attain, has resulted in better reception of fiction by first- and second-generation Americans. For instance, fiction by Bharati Mukherjee, who was born in Calcutta and earned a doctorate from the University of Iowa, includes *Darkness* (1985), *Jasmine* (1989), and *The Middleman and Other Stories* (1988) about Indian immigrants negotiating American culture. *Dreaming in Cuban* (1992), by Cristina Garcia, who was born in Havana and educated at Barnard College and Johns Hopkins University, tells the story of a Cuban family's flight from the Castro regime and their adjustment to the society of the United States. Gish Jen (*Typical American*, 1991) and Amy Tan (*The Joy Luck Club*, 1989; *The Kitchen God's Wife*, 1991) are second-generation Chinese-American writers; Jen was educated at Harvard and Stanford, Tan at San Jose State University. Both tell stories of acculturation, of forging a compromise between an old-world heritage and new-world opportunities.

---

[8] Note that the bibliography lists roughly a hundred titles under the thematic index "Focus on Women."

The final phase in the evolution of immigrant literature from a narrow special interest into a respected field of scholarly endeavor is its ability to define and design the terms upon which its study is undertaken. That is, beyond exposing nativist attitudes and stereotyped portrayals or recovering "lost" immigrant texts, scholars must address the literature on its own merit and construct critical methodologies for that purpose. This bibliography both chronicles and facilitates that changing face of immigrant literary criticism. For, in addition to citations of novels and short fiction, *The Immigrant Experience* includes selected criticism which, taken as a whole, reveals the dynamism of the genre's theoretical underpinnings. Scholarship from the 70s, when immigrant literary theory was just beginning to emerge, reflects that decade's emphasis on group-specific criticism. Thematic and historical studies such as Rose Basile Green's *The Italian-American Novel* (1974), Don Heinrich Tolzman's *German-American Literature* (1975), or Daniel Casey and Robert Rhodes' *Irish-American Fiction* (1979) examine only the writing of a particular group in isolation from others in order to outline the distinctiveness of the literature and to legitimate its authenticity.

As *The Immigrant Experience* illustrates, more recent scholarship challenges the earlier, separatist approach. For instance, Werner Sollors' *Beyond Ethnicity* (1986) and *The Invention of Ethnicity* (1989) and Jules Chametzky's *Our Decentralized Literature* (1986) identify important similarities as well as differences that exist in the fiction of different ethnic groups; they also reveal parallels between minority and majority writing. Sollors, William Boelhower, and other scholars advocate this transcultural approach to immigrant literature, the side-by-side study of fiction from different ethnic groups, rather than the earlier practice of examining a single group in isolation. The thematic index which concludes Professor Simone's bibliography is a useful aid to this kind of comparative study, making the commonalities as well as the divergences in experiences easily discernible. Adam Meyer goes one step further than Sollors and Boelhower by suggesting that the future of immigrant literary scholarship lies not just in observing parallels in the fiction by writers of different ethnic backgrounds, but also in cross-cultural criticism, which examines the intertextual conjunctions of people of varying nationalities.[9] The thematic index heading entitled "Inter-Ethnic Relations" will be helpful in studying these intersections. The thrust of the essays collected in Ruoff and

---

[9] Adam Meyer, "The Need for Cross-Ethnic Studies," *MELUS* 16.4 (1989-90): 19-39.

Ward's *Redefining American Literary History* (1990) is that the subjectivity of long-held notions of aesthetics needs to be addressed and the standards reconceived so as to recognize the fact of American diversity. Thomas Ferraro's *Ethnic Passages* (1993) addresses just such concerns by examining the "literariness"—the models and conventions—of the immigrant genre.

Most American literature survey courses now incorporate multi-cultural components, and a growing number of universities are implementing programs or even creating departments for ethnic studies. Clearly, much research has been done, yet much work remains. Taken as a whole, *The Immigrant Experience in American Fiction* provides assistance to students and scholars who seek a fuller account of the literary history of the United States.

Theresa Kanoza
Michigan State University

INTRODUCTION

When I was old enough, in the 1950s, to get a summer job in a local factory, I filled out applications which routinely asked for one's religion and nationality. For the latter, I always wrote down "Italian." It was not that I was unpatriotic: I had been educated in the public schools in my American heritage, and I had cheered for our troops throughout every World War II movie. But American was my citizenship; nationality meant what other country in the world your parents or other ancestors had come from, what distinguished you from other American citizens, what customs other than American ones had helped shape who you were and how you behaved.

Both of my parents were immigrants. I was born and grew up in an Italian immigrant community in Cicero, Illinois, an industrial town adjacent to Chicago. All around us, but separated by such urban borders as busy streets or bridges over railroad tracks, were other immigrant communities—Lithuanian, Czech, Polish, Dutch, Greek—and farther into the city were communities of seemingly every possible immigrant or other kind of ethnic group. Every American, I thought, had a nationality, and it was something to be proud of; it gave you a connection to some older and more exotic culture. I knew I was an American, but I thought I was also an Italian, even though I had never seen Italy—so strong was its culture in my family and community life.

The fifties were times of strong ethnic awareness, even of ethnic separateness; they were not times of tolerance for the ethnicity of others. Jokes about race, religion, and nationality abounded in ordinary conversations; stereotypes formed the basis of much popular entertainment. The civil rights movements of the sixties had a good deal to counteract. From them emerged ethnic pride among groups that had had little encouragement for it previously. Negroes became African-Americans, proclaiming their own connection to older and more exotic cultures and also pride in their race: "Black is beautiful." Hispanics, Asians, and Native Americans also demanded full citizenship rights and respect for their double cultures (as women did for their gender). Many "white ethnics," not to be outdone and showing that they had not melted in the great pot, responded with buttons and bumper stickers, announcing "Kiss me, I'm Irish" or "You bet your dupa I'm Polish." The metaphor of the melting pot as an ideal, offensive to many people anyway, was replaced with others which suggested unity without the loss of distinctions—the stew, the salad bowl, the quilt, and, especially, the mosaic.

Concurrently, there were demands for a more representative curriculum in education, one that included "minority" groups, a status that referred not only to race and gender, but to ethnicity as well. It was in that spirit and because of my lifelong interest in immigrants that I began to teach a new course at my university, The Immigrant Experience in America. It was conceived, at first, to be about European immigrants, since they seemed to be excluded from both mainstream and minority status. Surely they too deserved to be studied. A considerable body of historical and sociological scholarship was available for textbooks, as well as were biographies, autobiographies, and collections of memoirs. As an English professor, however, I wanted my students also to read fiction.

Immigrant fiction per se was not readily available. However, central to Rölvaag's *Giants in the Earth* (1927), which was generally described as a saga of the prairie, about pioneer life, is that those pioneers are Norwegian newcomers. Upton Sinclair's purpose in *The Jungle* (1906) was to expose the abuses of the meatpacking industry, but it also showed that those abuses had been perpetrated largely upon the immigrants who worked in it. Anzia Yezierska's stories were rediscovered by feminist scholars, but her characters were immigrants as well as women; and the novels of Abraham Cahan, Michael Gold, and Henry Roth, which Jewish-American literary scholarship had enabled to be reprinted, were as much about the immigrant as they were about the Jewish experience. Although not representative of many groups or historical periods, these books could form the core of a reading list in immigrant fiction.

The term "immigrants" often referred mainly to Europeans, as in Oscar Handlin's Pulitzer prize-winning *The Uprooted* (1951). Certainly, they had come in the largest numbers in the nineteenth and first half of the twentieth centuries. And they were Caucasians, like the earlier settlers (even if the older may have considered the newer ones inferior), and, therefore, eligible for citizenship and permanent residency. Non-Caucasian immigrants, on the other hand, were often thought of and treated merely as temporary workers who would willingly disappear after picking crops, canning fish, or building the railroads. Japanese-Americans, even native-born, were considered to be

Japanese during World War II and were made to disappear from West Coast cities.

Asians, Hispanics, and West Indians were generally being referred to as minorities, not immigrants. Yet it became increasingly clear to me that they should not be excluded from a course about immigrants, even if they were to be studied separately in Minority Literature courses, no more than should fiction by and about female immigrants (like that of Maxine Hong Kingston, Hisaye Yamamoto, Sandra Cisneros, Nicholasa Mohr, and Paule Marshall) even if it were being taught in Women's Literature courses. Moreover, contemporary writers needed to be included to remind us that waves of immigration have not ended, that new immigrants continue to become Americans.

The single most important goal in The Immigrant Experience course was for students to understand their own backgrounds and to make connections between the experiences of their ancestors and those of others. This goal necessitated my providing for them the resources by which they could accomplish it. That task was the motivation for the present bibliography.

"Is there a definition of ethnic literature with which we can be comfortable?" ask Robert J. Di Pietro and Edward Ifkovic in their *Ethnic Perspectives in American Literature: Selected Essays on the European Contribution* (1983), and then go on to illustrate that the answer appears to be negative (11-13). Werner Sollors offers a valuable rethinking of the meaning of ethnicity itself in *Beyond Ethnicity: Consent and Descent in American Culture* (1986). Immigrant fiction, however, may be easier to define. Since "ethnic" and "immigrant" fiction are genres that certainly overlap, I make a distinction on this basis: whereas ethnic fiction focuses on a particular group and is set in a dual culture, immigrant fiction, in addition, tells the story of becoming American.

The process of becoming American begins with making the choice to leave one's country to come to the United States—no simple matter to leave family, friends, and familiarity for the unknown. Some immigrants opted to make these sacrifices for a better life: more economic opportunity in the form of free or cheap land or better-paying jobs; or freedom from a class system; or the ability to establish one's own special church and community; or even for adventure. Yet many of the choices were forced ones. The desperately poor, the victims of political oppression or war may not have made a choice so much as taken an escape route from death. Children had to go along with their parents. The opinions of the wives of determined men may have counted for little: look, for instance, at Beret in *Giants in the Earth* (1927), who resisted her removal from Norway and, hating life in the Dakotas, could not persuade her husband, despite tears, silent withdrawal, and mad fits, to take the family back. Yet no one would deny Beret's status as an immigrant. Laborers who were being recruited by the railroad and steel companies were not always told the truth about their being able to earn big salaries and return home rich. The real choice of many such immigrant men was to come to the U.S. only temporarily. Many of those did indeed return to their homes. Others who had to stay may have cursed Columbus daily (like Michael Gold's father in *Jews Without Money*, 1930).

The completely involuntary immigrants, Africans captured and brought to the U.S. to be slaves, are not seen as immigrants at all. It is not for that reason alone that African-American literature is not included in this bibliography; the fiction of African-Americans is so extensive that it is an area for study of its own, in which many bibliographies and critical studies have already been published. The same may be said for the literature of Native Americans, who, clearly, by name alone cannot be identified as immigrants, unless one were to look at their original immigration, thousands of years ago, to the American continent (as Shawn Wong does in his novel *Homebase*, 1979). On the other hand, I have not considered for inclusion in this bibliography the fiction of the English and the Scots, although they were indeed those who first, and perhaps more freely than later immigrants, chose to settle in the lands occupied by the Native Americans. Regarding these first settlers, the element of choice is overriden by their having set the culture, which later comers would have to adapt to. The choice to immigrate, despite all these qualifications, remains a criterion in the definition of immigrant.

European immigrants, as has been noted, could choose to become American citizens; Asian immigrants, until World War II and after, could not; but all American-born children, regardless of background, were Americans legally by birth. All of these could yet choose whether or not and to what degree to become Americanized. All immigrants and their children have known the tug of war between maintaining old-world culture and customs and accepting the new American ones. For two very different examples, the children in Arnold Mulder's *The Dominie of Harlem* (1913) obediently go to their private church schools, learn to read the Dutch bible, and do not picnic on Sundays; whereas Hisaye Yamamoto's Rosie in "Seventeen Syllables" (*Seventeen Syllables and Other Stories*, 1988) skips Japanese language school to listen to Frank Sinatra on her bedroom radio. There is a cruel irony in these two examples: those Dutch immigrants could choose not to be "Americanized," but would still be considered Americans; Rosie, on the other hand, would continue to be classified, by other Americans, as Japanese. Such judgments continue: just recently, a fourth-generation Japanese-American professor at a large Western university noted in a public radio interview that he is consistently asked where he was born.

Complete assimilation was a possible choice for those who looked most like northern Europeans. Intermarriage between some European groups has blurred, even dissolved ethnic backgrounds; the grandchildren may know of these only from their several grandparents' accents and old photos or special ethnic dishes at a holiday dinner. Or the ethnic backgrounds might be too varied or too distant to be recognizable or significant at all. These people, apparently, have blended into the "mainstream," and, for them, the immigrant experience may have ended in the second generation.

Some groups, however, assimilable on the basis of physical features, could choose on religious grounds (as the Irish or Jews or the Pennsylvania Dutch) or political grounds (as the Cubans who waited for Castro's government to be overthrown) to maintain part of their culture and their separateness. For these, "ethnicity" is still related to their immigrant background.

The choice to assimilate becomes less possible as the differences from the physical model increase. For darker-skinned Caucasians and certainly for most non-Caucasians, the immigrant experience may extend to the fourth or fifth generation and beyond. If not by their own parents and grandparents, these are made constantly aware of their ancestry by others and are not allowed to forget it. Intermarriage between the races has not been extensive, not only because of anti-miscegenation laws, in existence in some states until the 1960s, but because of outgroup prejudices. The stories of these people are about still becoming American in the sense of being accepted as American by other Americans.

On the other hand, Americanization may be less a matter of conscious choice than of natural environmental adaptation. That is, by merely living in the United States, one can become Americanized. Two fictional illustrations come to mind. Serafino, in Helen Barolini's *Umbertina* (1979), returns to his home in Italy after working for several years at building the railroads in the United States. The villagers call him "l'americano," the American, because he "looked different. . . even in the way he acted. He walked differently, more freely." And Lindo Jong, in Amy Tan's *The Joy Luck Club* (1989), tells her grown-up daughter Waverly: "When you go to China. . . you don't even need to open your mouth. . . . Even if you put on their clothes, even if you take off your makeup and hide your fancy jewelry, they know. They know just watching the way you walk, the way you carry your face. . . ." Ironically, however much Serafino and Waverly might stand out as Americans abroad, at home they would be Italian and Chinese, respectively.

In the dual cultures in which immigrant fiction is set—the old country one in the new—each may be equally powerful. It is in this element that one might assume great differences in the fiction of the various immigrant groups. Indeed, the earliest bibliographies and critical works on the fiction of immigrant groups were done by members of the groups. Note Olga Peragallo, *Italian American Authors and their Contribution to American Literature* (1949) and Joseph Mersand, *Traditions in American Literature: A Study of Jewish Characters and Authors* (1939). That pattern continues in our own time, in which it is widely believed that only a member of the group can fairly assess the works by virtue of understanding, from having shared, the foreign culture which shaped them. From this, it may be further assumed that a specific immigrant novel will appeal to, will be read by, only members of the group.

However, pursuing such reasoning could also lead to such a conclusion as that only rural residents can appreciate farm settings in fiction, and only urban residents can appreciate city settings, only military veterans can be interested in Vietnam War fiction, and of those, only veterans of that specific war can truly understand it. The value of fiction has not been so much in having had the same experiences as do the characters in the novel, in being able, as students say, to "relate to" the characters. On the contrary, the value of fiction is that it enables us to enter another world, specifically, regarding immigrant fiction, into another culture. Fiction dramatizes for us the lives of others, through which we can make connections to our own.

Too much is made, I believe, of the differences in immigrant groups and not enough about their similarities. Reading immigrant fiction enables us to redress that imbalance. We have noted that immigrant fiction tells the story of balancing two cultures, however different one foreign background might be from another; it, therefore, also illustrates several common themes. For the first generation, for instance, initial shock; amused, embarrassed, even dishonest receptions by earlier immigrants of that group; hostility from and perhaps for other groups; homesickness and nostalgia; comparing the pros and cons of the old country and the new; beginning to make one's way through settlement and employment; dealing with children born in another land; deciding how much to give up of the old and how much to accept of the new. For the second generation, the prevailing theme is ambivalence: love and respect for parents but desire for individual freedom and new values; breaking away from familiarity but being lost outside the community; rejection and reconciliation. Stories of the third and fourth generations often involve the desire for connection with ancestors and their cultures. In all of these stories, the cultural details may change—the food, the terms, the old country heroes and legends, the religious observances, the special holidays—but the human elements do not. It is as possible to see immigrant fiction as a genre as it is to see groups of novels as belonging in ethnic divisions.

In this bibliography are some writings that others would classify as biography, autobiography, or memoirs. Especially in the stories of immigrants, these three genres may overlap. Because many readers refuse to believe that some stories are not based on actual incidents and people, novelists often preface their works with a notice that similarities are coincidental or must assure their parents and other relatives that characters, particularly unflattering portraits, are not meant to represent them. The protagonist in Jerre Mangione's *Mount Allegro* (1943) is Gerlando Amoroso, an indication that Mangione meant it to be perceived as fiction, yet it is often referred to as his memoirs, and some libraries shelve it as such. The characters in Hermann Hagedorn's *The Hyphenated Family* (1960) are Hermann and the Hagedorns, and the story is a straight description of the family's actual experiences, without, it would seem, much embellishment; yet he gave it the subtitle *A Novel*. A third example is *When Heaven and Earth Changed Places* (1989), in which Le Ly Hayslip makes no suggestions that it is other than an autobiography; yet the plot is so compelling and so ingeniously constructed, with its flashbacks and past-and-present parallels, and the characters are so fully developed that the book "reads," as least to me, more like a novel than do the other two.

Since these generic categories can be so hazy, and since a great many immigrant autobiographies exist, I decided to include autobiographical writings which seemed to be mostly based on a narrative structure. In particular, I thought it important to add these to immigrant groups that were underrepresented, as, for instance, Salom

Rizk's *Syrian Yankee* (1943) to the division "Syrian and Lebanese." To distinguish books of these sorts, I have included in the "Theme and Genre Index" the category "Fictionalized Autobiography," the term itself being broad and general enough, I hope, to account for books which not everybody would agree are strictly fiction.

The annotations of the bibliographical items are generally only descriptive of the contents, rather than critical or evaluative. Where critical works exist, they are listed under "Secondary Sources," and the reader is referred for critical judgments to these. Some ethnic groups have a considerable body of such works (e.g., Jewish, Hispanic, Asian, and the separate groups within the second two composite groups). I did not attempt to include all of them; rather, I refer the reader to the bibliographies listed under those divisions.

I did not exclude books because a critical judgment was negative, believing instead that the bibliography should be as comprehensive as possible. Indeed, as Paul Lauter explains in "The Literatures of America: A Comparative Discipline," in *Redefining American Literary History* (edited by Ruoff and Ward, New York: MLA, 1990), before we make critical judgments about marginalized writing in the United States, "We need to learn about, study, be sensitive to a far broader range of audiences, conventions, functions, histories and subjects than has in general been the case in literary analysis" (32). If some of the books in this bibliography may have been more motivated by the desire to record early experiences or to memorialize parents or grandparents than controlled by artistry, they are still important contributions to the cultural and sociological history of the U.S., a valuable resource for the student of immigrant culture and history. And they are also contributions to the study of American literature, filling in gaps not even thought formerly to be there. Significant critical works have been published recently about similarly ignored or forgotten fiction: e.g. Carol Fairbanks' *Prairie Women: Images in American and Canadian Fiction* (1986), and Laura Hapke's *Tales of the Working Girl: Wage-Earning Women in American Literature* (1992).

I did exclude books that were purported in a secondary source to be about the immigrant experience, but in actuality were nothing of the sort, rather were only written by a member of an immigrant group, using ethnic names for the characters (like the Polish Stella Rybacki's, *Thrills, Chills, and Sorrows*, 1954). I did not, for obvious reasons, include books which have not been translated into English; again, the reader is referred to the secondary sources to note that considerable body of literature. Though I have made every effort to be comprehensive through the first half of 1994, I regret any omissions that inevitably will be apparent.

For practical reasons, rather than to emphasize divisions, this bibliography is organized by immigrant group alphabetically, and further divided into works by individual authors, anthologies, secondary sources, and, where they exist, bibliographies. (The reader should note that some anthologies and secondary sources also include select bibliographies). Six composite groups are included within the alphabetical listing. These groupings indicate the tendency of some groups to unite under a commonality: of race (Asian), or native language (Hispanic), or related languages and geography (Scandinavian and Slavic) or colonial experience (West Indian) or religion and culture which override national origin (Jewish); and to publish collections of fiction under one cover or to treat the collective works critically.

A general category ends the bibliography. Here, one may note that interest in collective immigrant and ethnic literary works began in the public schools. Joseph Roucek compiled the bibliography *The Immigrant in Fiction and Biography* in 1945 for the Bureau for Intercultural Education; and Harry Shaw and Ruth Davis published the anthology of stories *Americans One and All* in 1947. Almost three decades later, in 1974, Katherine Newman founded the Society for the Study of Multi-Ethnic Literature of the United States and became the first editor of its journal, *MELUS*. A member of that society who was to become its second editor, Wayne C. Miller, compiled in 1976 *A Comprehensive Bibliography for the Study of American Minorities* as a resource for such scholarship. One can see from the growing number of books published since that time, in this category, the increasing attention being paid to commonalities among ethnic and immigrant literary works.

The "Theme and Genre Index" of the present bibliography is meant to implement that attention. Such sections as "Labor Union Activity," "Military Service," "Humor and Satire," and "Focus on Women," to name a few, will help the reader to find common elements among immigrant groups; "Settings" and "Employment" illustrate the full range of immigrant involvement in American life. "Young Adult Books" provides a listing of books that will appeal to young people. The "Index of Publication Dates" is meant to be an aid in tracing the historical patterns of writing by and about immigrants.

I wish here to acknowledge the assistance I have received in this project from the Grand Valley State University administration and librarians, from my colleague and friend, Lois Tyson, and from my longtime friend Theresa Kanoza, a fellow student of immigrant fiction. I am also grateful to Ginny Klingenberg for helping to prepare the manuscript.

THE BIBLIOGRAPHY

ARMENIAN

Individual Authors

1 Barba, Harry. *For the Grape Season*. New York: Macmillan, 1960.

Bachelor Bedros and his group of Armenian migrant workers come to Barstowe, Vermont to help the Yankees with the grape harvest. At first, both groups are suspicious of each other, but after intercultural love affairs, a wedding feast, and a three-day flood through which they all work together to survive, they come to understand and like each other.

2 Hagopian, Richard. *The Dove Brings Peace*. New York: Farrar and Rinehart, 1944.

Connected stories of the narrator Levon's growing up in an impoverished family, within an Armenian enclave, which exists among Italians and Irish in a shoe factory town in Massachusetts. His parents keep close to their relatives and friends, maintaining their cultural traditions and trying to prevent their children from becoming Americanized; in one incident they manage to break off their son Reuben's engagement to a non-Armenian woman.

3 ———. *Faraway the Spring*. New York: Scribner's, 1952.

Setrak Dinjyan, an immigrant shoemaker, and his wife Maryam, have lived in a Boston tenement for eighteen years, speak little English, and continue to feel like aliens in a foreign land; but they hope for better lives for their talented daughter, Sarah, and their crippled son, Vartan.

4 ———. *Wine for the Living*. New York: Scribner's, 1956.

Told from the point of view of the youngest son of the Aroian family, this is the story of their depressing home life, dominated by a cold and unforgiving mother who refuses to sanction the marriage of her children to non-Armenians and never relents after they go against her wishes.

5   Hoogasian-Villa, Susie. *One Hundred Armenian Tales and their Folkloristic Relevance.* Detroit: Wayne State University Press, 1966.

A collection of folktales which were circulating among the Armenian immigrant community in Detroit, and which, the collector notes, help keep their heritage alive and teach parallels to the adjustments necessary in their current lives.

6   Housepian, Marjorie. *A Houseful of Love.* New York: Random House, 1957.

An immigrant doctor's daughter tells humorous stories of growing up among her extended family of eccentric restaurateurs and shopkeepers in New York in the 1920s. The outstanding success is Uncle Levon Dai, who came to America carrying a few gallons of olive oil, became a wealthy importer of ethnic foods, traveled all over the United States, and married into an old New England family.

7   Najorian, Peter. *Daughters of Memory.* Berkeley, CA: City Miner Books, 1986.

Zeke's mother is orphaned by the Turks in Armenia and can't remember her mother. She never tells her American-born son Zeke about the Armenian genocide and that those who are in America came as refugees. Instead, he learns this information from some old women in his neighborhood. Much moved, he goes, when an adult, to Turkey to find his grandmother's village and come to terms with his double heritage.

8   ———. *Voyages.* New York: Pantheon Books, 1971.

Petrus and Melina Tomasian live with the guilt of being survivors of the Armenian genocide. Their son Aram cannot reconcile his parents' past with his American identity and resents his brother Yero's successful economic and emotional assimilation. To avoid the same fate, he goes to London, but feels alienated there. Finally, he faces his dilemma and is able to rid himself of his own sense of guilt.

9   Saroyan, William. *Madness in the Family.* Edited by Leo Hamalian. New York: New Directions, 1988.

Stories, published posthumously in this collection, originally published in magazines in the 1960s and 1970s, about half of which are about the Armenian immigrant community in Fresno.

10   ————. *My Name Is Aram.* New York: Harcourt, Brace, 1940.

Suitable for young adults. Aram Garoghlanian tells humorous and poignant stories about growing up in an impoverished Armenian immigrant family in Fresno, California, and of his eccentric relatives: e.g., Uncle Melik, who tries to grow pomegranate trees in the desert, and cousin Dikran, who fancies himself a great orator.

11   ————. *Rock Wagram.* New York: Doubleday, 1951.

Arak Vagranian is brought up in the Armenian community of Fresno by his immigrant parents and grandmother, who cling to their Armenian culture and memories of the devastation of their homeland. Arak calls himself a bad Armenian because he cannot sufficiently hate, as his parents do, their old world enemies, the Turks, and is unwilling to work for his father editing an Armenian newspaper. While working as a bartender, he is offered a career in film. Arak changes his name to Rock Wagram, goes to Hollywood, becomes a famous romantic lead, and marries a young starlet; but he cannot overcome his guilt over having left his home and heritage, and his marriage fails.

12   Sourian, Peter. *The Gate.* New York: Harcourt, Brace and World, 1965.

Vahan Stepanyan is the only member of his family to escape the Turkish massacre in his village. His son Sarkis comes to America, bringing up his son Paul with no knowledge of his Armenian heritage. Paul does research on Armenian history and wants to write the story of his father's life. An architect, he also designs the new Armenian cathedral in New York.

13   Surmelian, Leon. *I Ask You, Ladies and Gentlemen.* New York: Dutton, 1945.

An autobiographical novel about a young man who is uprooted from Armenia during the Turkish massacres. He escapes to Russia and then comes to study at the University of Kansas. He has a hard time adjusting to American life, particularly as he remembers the plight of his people in Armenia. He visits New York, and on New Year's Eve, writes passionately of his gratitude to the United States as a country he would willingly fight for. Yet he can't forget that Armenia is his true homeland and asks the "ladies and gentlemen" of the United States to help his people.

Anthologies

14 Antreassin, Jack, ed. *Ararat: A Decade of Armenian-American Writing.* New York: Armenian General Benevolent Union, 1969.
   Selections of essays, drama, poetry and fiction from a quarterly journal begun in 1959 to encourage Armenian-American writers. The section of fiction includes stories by William Saroyan, Peter Sourian, Leon Surmelian, Kathryn Manoogian, Vaughn Koumijian, Harry Barba, and David Tutaev.

15 Hamalian, Leo, ed. *Ararat: 25th Anniversary Special.* New York: Armenian General Benevolent Union, 1985.
   An updated collection of the same kinds of writings that appear in the 1969 publication.

16 *Three Worlds: Hairenik, 1934-1939.* Boston: Hairenik Press, 1939. Reprint, Freeport, NY: Books for Libraries, 1971.
   With an introduction by William Saroyan. A collection of poems, sketches and stories from a weekly newsletter (whose title means "fatherland"), instituted to be a vehicle for young Armenian writers. Divided into three sections—"The Old World," "The New World," and "The Coming World." The second section contains stories about the immigrant experience. John Melikian's "The Thin Slice of Ham" is about growing up fatherless and suffering through the rigidities of the public school. Varon Kalyan's "My Grandfather's God" concerns a boy's remembrance of his grandfather's execution in the old country for not converting to Islam. In Azad Mamigonian's "Khetcho," two fathers worry about the Americanization of their sons at the wedding of a young man who has done right by marrying an Armenian woman. And Hrant K. Armen's "The Son" is about a shoemaker in Boston who advertises in international newspapers for his son, separated from him in the Turkish massacres.

Secondary Sources

17 Balakian, Nona. *The Armenian-American Writer: A New Accent in American Fiction.* New York: Armenian General Benevolent Union, Random House, 1958.

A discussion of the literary contributions of Armenian-American writers, beginning with an explanation of how these writers have had to integrate their national past into the alien world in which they came to live. William Saroyan, the best and best known, speaks for them all, she says, in his dedication to the English language and to the American homeland and spirit. She reviews his achievements and those of others who follow his lead in their depiction of Armenian-American life: Surmelian, Hagopian, and Housepian. The book includes annotated bibliographies, biographical sketches, and literary criticism.

18 ———. "Armenian Ethnic Literature of the United States." *Ethnic Literatures Since 1776: The Many Voices of America.* Eds., Wolodymyr T. Zyla and Wendell M. Aycock: Lubbock: Proceedings of the Comparative Literature Symposium, Texas Tech University, Jan. 1976. IX (1978): I, 49-69.

A historical and critical survey, beginning with a discussion of William Saroyan, who, through using his Armenian background to illustrate his belief in the goodness of people and through his humor, irony, and refusal to be bitter, led the way for Surmelian, Hagopian, Najorian, and other Armenian-American writers of fiction to keep alive a compassionate view of human nature in American writing.

19 Bedrosian, Margaret. *The Magical Pine Ring: Culture and the Imagination in Armenian-American Literature.* Detroit: Wayne State University Press, 1991.

The introduction is a historical and cultural survey of the Armenian people, both in the old countries and as refugees in America, which leads to a discussion of their literature: that written by the children of immigrants is the "most compelling" in that it has been "directed by a vision through cultural bi-focals." Eleven essays on individual writers follow, including Saroyan, Sourian, Najorian, and Hagopian.

20 Shirinian, Lorne. *Armenian-North American Literature: A*

Critical Introduction: Genocide, Diaspora and Symbols. Lewiston, NY: Mellen, 1990.

A historical and cultural background to Armenian-American literature, mainly fiction, particularly as it deals with reactions to the massacres of Armenians in 1915 and after. Special attention is given to Saroyan, Najorian, and Sourian.

ASIAN (see also Burmese, Chinese, Filipino, Indian, Japanese, Korean, and Vietnamese)

Anthologies

21 Asian Women United of California, eds. *Making Waves: An Anthology of Writings by and about Asian American Women.* Boston: Beacon Press, 1989.

Mostly historical and autobiographical essays and poetry, but some fiction. Chinese: Nellie Wong, "Broad Shoulders." Filipino: Cecilia Manguerra Brainard, "Waiting for Papa's Return," and Virginia Cerenio, "Dreams of Manong Frankie." Indian: Kartor Dhillon, "The Parrot's Beak," and Meena Alexander, "Mosquitoes in the Main Room." Japanese: R. A. Sasaki, "The Loom," Wakako Yamauchi, "Makapuu Bay," and Valerie Matsumoto, "Two Deserts." Korean: Elaine H. Kim, "War Story," and K. Kam, "The Hopeland."

22 Chiang, Fay, Helen Wong Huie, Jason Jwang, Richard Oyama, and Susan L. Yung, eds. *American Born and Foreign.* New York: Sunbury Press, 1979.

An anthology of Chinese- and Japanese-American writings.

23 Chin, Frank, Jeffrey Paul Chan, Lawson Fusao Inada, and Shawn Wong, eds. *Aiiieeeee!: An Anthology of Asian-American Writers.* Washington, D.C.: Howard University Press, 1974. Reprint, NY: Mentor, 1991.

Includes fiction by Chinese-Americans Jeffrey Chan, Louis Chu, and Shawn Wong; Filipino-Americans Carlos Bulosan and Sam Tagatec; and Japanese-Americans Hisaye Yamamoto, Wakako Yamauchi, John Okada and Momoko Ito. The introductory essay is on the history of Asian-Americans as presented in fiction, with the intent of dispelling the stereotypes of the mysterious and cunning Asians and replacing them with characters and experiences which are true to Asian-Americans, which were formerly rejected by American publishers as having insufficient interest for the mainstream reader.

24 ————. *The Big Aiiieeeee! An Anthology of Chinese-American and Japanese-American Literature.* New York: Mentor, 1991.

Twice the size of the original anthology, it adds several new writers, including poets, but only Chinese and Japanese. The historical approach begins with the very first writings by Asian-Americans—e.g., "An English-Chinese Phrase Book" and a story by Sui Sin Far—and goes on to include both established (Shawn Wong, Kazuo Miyamoto, Toshio Mori, Monica Sone, Milton Murayama, Hisaye Yamamoto, John Okada, Louis Chu, and David Wong Louie) and new and less known writers. Chin's new and longer introduction, "Come All Ye Asian-American Writers of the Real and the Fake," analyzes past fiction in the light of its authenticity and calls upon Asian-American writers to continue to repudiate stereotypes of their groups in fiction and to insist on their place in American literature.

25 Gee, Emma, ed. *Counterpoint: Perspectives on Asian America.* Los Angeles: Asian-American Studies Center at the University of California, 1976.

An anthology of fiction and essays, including stories by Frank Chin, Shawn Hsu Wong, and others.

26 Hagedorn, Jessica, ed. *Charlie Chan Is Dead: An Anthology of Contemporary Asian American Fiction.* New York: Penguin Books, 1993.

In the preface, Elaine Kim says that this anthology "celebrates many ways of being Asian and American today" in that one must no longer be one or the other. Hagedorn's introduction gives a brief history of Asian-American writing. The collection contains forty-eight fiction pieces, almost half by those never before published in a major anthology. Those better known are the older writers Toshio Mori, Bienvenido Santos, Maxine Hong Kingston, and Hisaye Yamamoto, and the new generation: Bharati Mukherjee, Gish Jen, Sylvia Watanabe, Fay Myenne Ng, David Wong Louie, and Cynthia Kadohata. Ethnic groups represented are Chinese, Filipino, Hawaiian, Indian, Indonesian, Japanese, Korean, Pakistani, and Vietnamese.

27 Hsin-Fu Wand, David, ed. *Asian American Heritage.* New York: Washington Square Press, 1974.
An anthology of fiction, essay, and poetry by Chinese-, Japanese-, and Korean-American writers.

28 Hsu, Kai-yu and Helen Palubinskas, eds. *Asian-American Authors.* Boston: Houghton, Mifflin, 1972.
One of the earliest of the Asian-American anthologies, it contains an introductory essay of a general nature as well as brief introductions to Chinese-, Japanese-, and Filipino-American literature. In addition to poetry and essays is relevant fiction by the Chinese, Virginia Lee, Frank Chin, Diana Chang, and Jeffrey Chan; Japanese, Toshio Mori and Hisaye Yamamoto; and Filipino, Bienvenido Santos.

29 Planas, Alvin, Kevin Yuen, Elaine Becker, and Neal La Schele, eds. *Hanai: An Anthology of Asian American Writings.* Berkeley: University of California Press, Asian Studies Department, 1980.

30 Tachiki, Amy, et al. *Roots: An Asian American Reader.* Los Angeles: Asian American Studies Center at the University of California, 1971.
An anthology of fiction and essays.

31 Watanabe, Sylvia and Carol Bruchac, eds. *Home to Stay: Asian-American Women's Fiction.* Greenfield Center, NY: Greenfield Review Press, 1990.
Stories by first-, second-, and third-generation immigrants. Chinese: Maxine Hong Kingston, Gish Jen, Sara J. Lau, Wen-Wen C. Wang, Fae Myenne Ng, Amy Tan, and Sussy Chako. Filipino: Cecilia Manguerra Brainard, Jessica Hagedorn, and Linda Ty-Casper. Indian: Meena Alexander, Chitra Divakaruni, Arun Mukherjee, and Bharati Mukherjee. Japanese: Marie M. Hora, Tina Kayama, Susan Nunes, Wakako Yamauchi, Rosanna Yamagiwa Alfaro, Hisaya Yamamoto, Mavis Hara, Sharon Hashimoto, and Sylvia Watanabe. Malaysian: Shirley Geok-lin Lim. Pakistani: Tahira Naqvi. Vietnamese: Elizabeth Gordon.

Secondary Sources

32 *Asian Perspectives. MELUS* 18:4, Winter, 1993.

Pertinent articles are on Maxine Hong Kingston, Jessica Hagedorn, Louie Chu and Diana Chang, and an interview with Gish Jen.

33 Geok-lin Lim, Shirley. "Twelve Asian American Writers: In Search of Self-Definition." *Redefining American Literary History.* Eds. A. LaVonne Brown Ruoff and Jerry W. Ward, Jr. New York: MLA, 1990. 237-51.

Distinguishes between such early writers of fiction as Lin Yutang and Virginia Lee, who relied on stereotypes; Okada and Chu, who, in attempting to be more authentic, wrote protest literature with "manly" protagonists; and Kingston, Mori and Diana Chang, whose stronger works offer "alternative self-images to the ethnic commonplaces that substitute for phenomenological texture."

34 Geok-lin Lim, Shirley, and Amy Ling, eds. *Reading the Literatures of Asian America.* Philadelphia: Temple University Press, 1992.

Twenty critical essays on Asian-American literature in general and specific essays on Chinese-, Filipino-, Japanese-, Hawaiian/Asian Pacific-, Indian-, and Vietnamese-American writers.

35 Kim, Elaine H. *Asian-American Literature: An Introduction to the Writings and their Social Context.* Philadelphia: Temple University Press, 1982.

A comprehensive, socio-historical and cultural study of Asian-American images in American literature, and, from its beginnings to its "new directions" in the 1980s, of Asian-American writing in English, with special attention to Chinese writers Lin Yu Tang, Chin Yang Lee, Louis Chu, Maxine Hong Kingston, Frank Chin, Jeffrey Paul Chan, and Shawn Hsu Wong; Japanese writers Toshio Mori, Milton Murayama, John Okada, and Hisaye Yamamoto; Korean writers Younghill Kang; and Filipino writers Carlos Bulosan and Bienvenido Santos. It includes excellent notes with references to collections in journals and an extensive bibliography of primary and secondary works.

36 ———. "Defining Asian-American Realities through Literature." *Cultural Critique* 6 (Spring, 1987): 87-111.

A historical survey of Asian-Americans presented as foreign images in literature and as writers who have been expressing their "'otherness' not as foreigners but as American 'others.'" Attention is given to the Burmese writer Wendy Law-Yone and the Filipinos Sam Tagatec and Carlos Bulosan, as well as to Chinese and Japanese writers.

37   Sau-ling, Cynthia Wong. *Reading Asian American Literature: From Necessity to Extravagance.* Princeton, NJ: Princeton University Press, 1993.

This book examines four motifs that recur in distinct patterns in Asian-American fiction and cross the boundaries of gender, class, generation, and history: food, double identity, mobility, and play. One chapter is devoted to Maxine Hong Kingston and there is concentration on Chinese (Frank Chin, David Wong Louie, Fae Myenne Ng, Amy Tan, and Shawn Wong) and Japanese (Toshio Mori, Monica Sone, Yoshiko Uchida, Hisaye Yamamoto, and Wakako Yamauchi); but Filipinos Carlos Bulosan and Bienvenido Santos, and the Indian Bharati Mukherjee are also examined.

Bibliographies

38   Cheung, King-Kok, and Stan Yogi. *Asian American Literature: An Annotated Bibliography.* New York: MLA, 1988.

Primary and secondary works, with selected literature for children and young adults.

39   Ling, Amy. "Asian American Literature, a Bibliography." *Redefining American Literary History.* Eds., A. LaVonne Brown Ruoff and Jerry W. Ward, Jr. New York: MLA, 1990.

Includes anthologies, primary and secondary works, and works on individual authors by Chinese-, Japanese-, Korean-, Filipino-, and Southeast Asian-American writers.

BASQUE

Individual Authors

40   Isasi, Mirim. *Basque Girl.* Illustrated by Kurt Wiese. Glendale, CA: Griffin-Patterson, 1940.

For young adults. A girl tells about her life coming and adjusting to the United States.

41 Isasi, Mirim, and Melcena Burns Denny. *White Stars of Freedom.* Niles, IL: Whitman, 1942.
For young adults. A boy tells of the adventures he undergoes in migrating to California.

42 Laxalt, Robert. *Sweet Promised Land.* New York: Harper and Brothers, 1957.
Dominique leaves his Pyrenees village at age sixteen in 1908 to be a sheepherder in the Sierra Nevada mountains. In the 1929 crash Dominique loses the great flock of sheep he has come to own and starts again as a hired herder, refusing to live and work anywhere but in the mountains, while his wife cares for their six children and runs a small hotel in Carson City. When he is past sixty and his adult children have all become successful in professions, son Robert, the narrator, accompanies him on a visit to his Pyrenees family and records the stories his father tells of his youth in France, his emigration, and the experiences of the Basque immigrant shepherds in Nevada, including violent territorial wars with cattlemen.

BURMESE (see also Asian)

Individual Authors

43 Law-Yone, Wendy. *The Coffin Tree.* New York: Knopf, 1983.
The daughter and son of a military officer in Rangoon escape the Communist takeover after World War II and come alone to New York to find an American acquaintance of their father. The cold weather and their alienation in the totally new environment lead to the son's mental breakdown, but the sister is able, slowly, to adjust and to earn a living for both of them.

CHINESE (see also Asian)

Individual Authors

44 Bezine, Yun Ching. *Children of the Pearl.* New York: Signet, 1991.

Four young people from South China come in 1911 to San Francisco: Sung Quamming is going to join his uncle's prosperous trading company; Li Fachai, son of a poor fisherman plans to work in a fish processing plant; the recently orphaned fourteen-year-old Fong Loone is being sent by his uncle to make a new life for himself; and Yung Meiping's father has, against her knowledge, sold her to a house of prostitution. During the next twenty years, the lives of these four intersect in Chinatown as they learn to deal with violence and racial prejudice.

45   ———. *On Wings of Destiny*. New York: Signet, 1993.
A group of young people flee to the U.S. after the Communist takeover in 1949.

46   ———. *Temple of the Moon*. New York: Signet, 1992.
A sequel to *Children of the Pearl*, about the three survivors and their children, living through the 1930s and 1940s.

47   Cao, Glen. *Beijinger in New York*. Translated by Ted Wang. San Francisco: Cypress Book Co., 1993.
Wang Qiming, cellist, and Guo Yan, violinist, husband and wife, are successful in getting visas to the U.S., but they must leave their eleven-year-old daughter Ning Ning in Beijing with relatives. In New York, he is bitterly disappointed by his Chinese sponsor's refusal to help him find decent housing or a job. Wang finds work as a dishwasher, but through hard work and a heavy mortgage eventually owns a sweater factory. Ning Ning arrives as a teenager and is lured to the street life of the young drug crowd. Wang nearly loses his factory because of corrupt lawyers and business associates and does lose his daughter. These experiences harden him to the plight of new arrivals from China.

48   Chao, Evalina. *Gates of Grace*. New York: Warner, 1985.
Mei-yu and Kung-chiau manage to get the last boat out of Canton Harbor as the revolutionary communist troops storm Peking. Their child Fernadina (Sing-hua) is born in Chinatown in San Francisco. Kung-chiau becomes a victim of the political and economic warfare of the immigrant Chinese in the city. Aided by Madame Peng, one of the business leaders, Mei-yu takes her child to Washington, D.C., where they become part of the social scene connected to the Chinese embassy, and Mei-yu marries Richard

Peng, a prominent lawyer. Fernadina misses the Chinatown community and stands out in the mostly white suburb in which she lives, but when she is a student at Columbia University, she is able to rejoin the Chinatown society in New York without feeling any less American.

49   Chin, Frank. *The Chinaman Pacific and Frisco R.R. Co.* Minneapolis: Coffee House, 1988.

Humorous satirical stories set in the Chinese-American community in Oakland, California, where the people try to accommodate themselves to white food, music and movies while hanging on to their own values and customs. Chin's satire attempts to break down the stereotypes of earlier images of Chinese-Americans in fiction.

50   ———. *Donald Duk.* Minneapolis: Coffee House, 1991.

Told with wry humor is this story of eleven-year-old Donald, who lives in San Francisco's Chinatown and works part-time at his father's restaurant. He is embarrassed by his Chineseness—his father King, his mother Daisy—and idolizes American movie stars, especially Fred Astaire. His uncle, a famous Cantonese opera star, and his father teach him to appreciate his culture by way of Chinese myths and Chinese-American heroes, like Kwan, the foreman in the laying of the railroads. He accepts his heritage when he can see it clearly and free of stereotypes.

51   Chu, Louis. *Eat a Bowl of Tea.* New York: Lyle Stuart, 1961. Reprint, Seattle: University of Washington Press, 1979.

Ben Loy, an immigrant's son and a World War II veteran, goes to China to visit his mother and to find a wife. He brings Mei Oi to New York's Chinatown, where the mostly male community take a special interest in the couple's sexual progress and are concerned about her inability to become pregnant. When she does, the child is not her husband's, and there is shame over the scandal. The once friendly fathers of the couple leave town, and the couple nearly divorce. Instead, they move to San Francisco and plan to reconcile with their fathers. A film is based on this novel.

52   Chuang Hua. *Crossings.* Boston: Northeastern University Press, 1986.

The family of a Chinese surgeon escape the Communist takeover and take refuge in England and then New York. During the Korean War, they have conflicts in loyalty for their two countries. Jane, the fourth of the seven children, has further conflicts between her loyalty to her father and her married, European lover, which are symbolized by her frequent flights, "crossings," between Paris and New York.

53 Far, Sui Sin [Edith Eaton]. *Mrs. Spring Fragrance.* Chicago: McClurg, 1912.
    Stories, some for young adults, about the Chinese and Eurasians in California at the turn of the century. One of the earliest works to show Asians realistically and sympathetically.

54 Jen, Gish. *Typical American.* Boston: Houghton Mifflin, 1991.
    Yifeng comes in 1947 to study in a New York university, changing his name to Ralph. When the Communists take over the government in China, he drops out of school and hides, afraid that he will be considered an enemy alien. His refugee sister Theresa finds him and assures him that he can continue his studies, which he does, earning a Ph.D. in Engineering and eventually getting a tenure-track teaching job. But, persuaded by his friend Grover Ding that he can become wealthy, and attempting to satisfy the American suburban tastes of his Chinese wife Helen (who had accompanied Theresa to New York) and their two daughters, he buys a fried chicken restaurant.

55 Kingston, Maxine Hong. *China Men.* New York: Knopf, 1980.
    Historical stories, set between the mid-nineteenth century and the present, in which the protagonists are the author's male ancestors and other relatives made to represent the generic Chinese immigrants and their experiences: e.g., great-grandfather working on Hawaiian plantations; grandfather building the railroads; and brother serving in the U.S. Army.

56 ———. *Tripmaster Monkey: His Fake Book.* New York: Knopf, 1991.
    In this novel full of word play and "in-jokes" of the San Francisco Chinese-American community, Wittman Ah Song, a graduate from Berkeley in the sixties, continually expresses his anger over the treatment of Asian-Americans in the arts,

particularly in theater and film. He writes poetry and dreams of writing and staging a long drama made up of several interwoven Chinese classical stories, one in which Asian-Americans can play the roles of heroes and ordinary people rather than stereotypes. After losing his job, marrying, and searching for his grandmother, he does stage a play, and he urges the actors, writers and audience to continue to demand just treatment in the arts, including real parts in plays instead of stereotyped roles.

57   ————. *The Woman Warrior: Memoirs of a Girlhood Among Ghosts.* New York: Knopf, 1976.

A girl grows up in San Francisco's Chinatown, attending both public and Chinese schools and trying to be both American and Chinese. In explaining the confusion of roles that haunts her even as a grown woman, she tells the stories she learned from her mother while growing up: e.g., of an aunt who had disgraced the family by bearing a child not her husband's and committed suicide; of her mother's attending medical school; and of a legendary woman warrior and hero. As well, she recounts the difficulties of growing up with a mother whose cryptic messages to her are alternately to be passive and resigned to fate or to be strong and assertive.

58   LaPlere, Richard Tracy. *Where the Living Strive.* New York: Harper and Brothers, 1941.

For young adults. A story of immigrant life in San Francisco, describing customs and lifestyles at the end of the nineteenth century and the beginning of the twentieth.

59   Lee, Chin Yang. *Flower Drum Song.* New York: Farrar, Strauss and Cudahy, 1957.

A comic tale about Wang Chi-Yang, a wealthy immigrant from Taiwan, who lives in San Francisco's Chinatown, speaking only Chinese, eating only Chinese food, and, in general, living as he did in China. His son, Wang Ta, angers his father by living like a typical American—e.g., eating sandwiches and playing ball. But When Wang Ta falls in love with and wants to marry a pretty, recent immigrant from China, he takes his father's life-style more seriously.

60   ———. *The Land of the Golden Mountain*. New York: Meredith,
      1967.
          The unlikely, romantic tale of a Chinese girl, Mai Mai, from a
      village near Canton, who, to escape the famines of the 1840s,
      disguises herself as a boy in order to dig for gold in the mountains
      east of San Francisco. Aboard ship, the Chinese protest burials at
      sea and the greasy Western food which they are compelled to eat.
      At work in the mines, they protest the underpayment for and
      dangers of their work. Mai Mai had planned to find enough gold
      to return to China with wealth, but she falls in love with her
      American employer, decides to marry him and become an
      American citizen.

61   Lee, Gus. *China Boy*. New York: Dutton, 1992.
          Kei Ting is the only son of an aristocratic Shanghai family
      which has fled from China in 1944, after Mao's Communist
      revolution. His father just manages to support the family with his
      job at a San Francisco bank, and Kei Ting, in the 1950s, must
      learn to survive on the tough streets of a mixed ethnic
      neighborhood. In this he is aided by boxing lessons from the local
      YMCA and lessons in Chinese wisdom by Uncle Shim, the
      Mandarin Scholar.

62   Lee, Virginia. *The House that Tai Ming Built*. New York:
      Macmillan, 1963.
          Bo Lin grows up with her grandfather, an immigrant who
      teaches her pride in her ethnic heritage, and her parents in San
      Francisco's Chinatown. She falls in love with Scott Hayes, but
      miscegenation laws in the early 1940s prevent their marriage, and
      he dies fighting in Europe in World War II.

63   Leong, Monfoon. *Number One Son*. San Francisco: East/West,
      1975.
          Chuck Chan's biographical introduction explains that the book
      was published posthumously because it was repeatedly rejected
      on the grounds that it would not appeal to the "mainstream." The
      longest story, "Precious Jade," is about a young woman who is
      taken from China by her uncle to San Francisco to marry a labor
      medium for constructing the American railroads. In anti-Chinese
      riots, her husband is killed. Other stories, all set in California, are
      "A Good Burial," about Uncle Wing Koon, who wishes to buy a

mound, not merely a plot and a headstone, under which to bury his wife; "Youth for Kwam Kim," about an old man who believes that with an old country potion he can be young again, marry, and have a child; "New Year for Fong Wing," in which a father grieving for his dead soldier son befriends a legless young veteran; "Uncle's Monkey," in which Uncle Kim, the herbalist, teaches his nephew, with old country "magic," how to win the approval of the father of the rich, white young woman whom he wants to marry; "Herb Tea for Grandmother Wong," concerning a ten-year-old who thinks herbal tea can save his grandmother from dangerous surgery; and the title story, in which a young man, angry at having to live in poverty because of his overly generous father, comes to respect his father after his death.

64 Lin Yu Tang. *Chinatown Family.* New York: Day, 1948.

The Fongs are presented as ideal immigrants who can blend both the old culture and the new. They work in their own laundry and then restaurant business in the 1930s. Although they maintain their Chinese rituals, holidays, and celebrations, as well as the tenets of Confucianism and Taoism and traditional family structure in which children obey and support their parents, they manage at the same time to adapt to Christianity and American business procedures and cultural ideals. Although father Tom is killed in a car accident, the driver's "guilt money" reinforces their faith in a kind America.

65 Louie, David Wong. *Pangs of Love.* New York: Knopf, 1991. Reprint, New York: Plume, 1992.

Eleven stories about the conflicts for the second generation over their two heritages, compounded by their physical inability to blend into the American scene. In "Birthday," Wallace Wong refuses to marry a Chinese woman and give up his obsession with a white woman and her son. In "Displacement," Mrs. Chow, the highly educated wife of a Nationalist Army officer, pretends not to know English or to understand the criticisms of the rich widow, for whom she and her husband are maid and handyman. "Inheritance" concerns second generation Edna, who values Chinese customs and is a peace activist during the Vietnam War, though her husband, a recent refugee from Communist China, supports the war and is enthusiastic about mainstream American culture. The title story is about Mrs. Pang and her two sons, neither of whom will accept their mother's wish to arrange their marriages with women from Hong Kong. She remains oblivious to what their lives as Americans are really like, because she lives a totally Chinese life in New York's Chinatown.

66 McCunn, Ruthanne Lum. *Thousand Pieces of Gold.* San Francisco: Design Enterprises, 1981.

A novel based on the life of Lalu Nathoy (1853-1933), who was stolen in 1870, at eighteen, from her family in China by bandits. They sell her to a house of prostitution, from which she is shipped to San Francisco to be a prostitute there. She is bought by a saloon keeper in an Oregon mining town and then won in a poker game by Jim Bemis, whom she eventually marries and with whom she becomes a homesteader in Idaho.

67 Ng, Fae Myenne. *Bone.* New York: Hyperion, 1993.

A story of two generations of Chinese-Americans in San Francisco's Chinatown. Mah has worked hard for years in garment sweatshops, and her husband, Leung, a former merchant shipman, has worked double shifts in ships' laundries in order for them to support their children. These children disappoint their parents in their desires to be like other Americans. Each wishes to leave the confines of the family and Chinese community. Leila moves to the suburbs and Nina to New York. Ona, who cannot reconcile desire for independence with that for security, commits suicide; and Leon, their "paper son," does not keep his promise to take old Leung's bones back to China.

68 Pinkwater, Manus. *Wingman.* New York: Dodd, Mead, 1975.

For young adults. A Chinese-American immigrant boy experiencing conflicts in his school withdraws into his own world of fantasy, until his teacher helps him to gain pride in who he is.

69 Tan, Amy. *The Joy Luck Club.* New York: Putnam's, 1989.

A bestseller which did much to bring Chinese immigrant life to the attention of the mainstream reading public. It is made up of sixteen connected stories told by four Chinese women (Suyuan Woo, An Mei Hsu, Lindo Jong, and Ying Ying St. Clair) who immigrate to California just after World War II, and by their four American born daughters (Jing-mei "June" Woo, Rose Hsu, Waverly Jong, and Lena St. Clair). The mothers' stories are about their childhoods in China and their struggles to raise their daughters to take full advantage of the opportunities for women in America and yet not to forget their Chinese heritage; the four daughters tell of the conflicts in their own lives by growing up in the two cultures of Chinatown in San Francisco. Though resisting the Chinese wisdom of their mothers, the daughters are also shaped by and come to value it: e.g., June visits her family in China to understand her roots. A 1993 film is based on the novel.

70 ———. *The Kitchen God's Wife*. New York: Putnam's, 1991.

The story of a woman's horrifying experiences in World War II China as the wife of a corrupt and cruel military officer and her escape to the United States through marriage to an American citizen; the daughter learns of her mother's past only when she is an adult and facing a debilitating disease. She is married to a Caucasian, and her own children have known about their Chinese heritage only from the occasional family celebrations which they attend.

71 Telemaque, Eleanor Wong. *It's Crazy to Stay Chinese in Minnesota*. Nashville, TN: Thomas Nelson, 1978.

Seventeen-year-old Ching, the daughter of restaurant owners in a small town in which there are very few Chinese, admires her honest father and the young Chinese man Bingo, who teaches her about China and the history of Chinese in America. But finally she must struggle herself with racial discrimination and finding her own identity.

72 Wong, Jade Snow. *Fifth Chinese Daughter*. New York: Harper and Brothers, 1950.

An autobiographical account of a young woman's struggles with her family's expectations for her to live the traditional life of a Chinese woman. She, however, wants to be an artist, and, eventually, she accomplishes her goals.

73 Wong, Shawn. *Homebase*. New York: I Reed Books, 1979.

A young man tries to experience in his imagination the life of his great-grandfather, who came in the 1860s to build the railroad, including his detention at Angel Island. In so doing, he feels a kinship with Native Americans, whose ancestors immigrated to America from China 30,000 years earlier.

74   Yep, Laurence. *Dragon's Gate*. New York: Harper Collins, 1993.
     For young adults. In the 1860s, Otter lives with his adoptive
     father Uncle Foxfire, who is fighting against the Manchu
     conquerors. They plan to go to the U.S., learn its latest technology
     and return to China to continue their fight. But the boy must flee
     on his own. He joins his real father, who is building the railroad
     in the Sierra Nevadas. With him he learns that his uncle is not a
     real hero, and he decides to stay with his father.

75   ———. *Dragonwings*. New York: Harper and Row, 1975.
     For young adults. The boy Moonshadow immigrates to San
     Francisco, where his father operates a laundry and, as a hobby,
     makes wonderful kites. Although undergoing discriminatory
     treatment by white Americans, Moonshadow takes pleasure in
     helping his father build a flying machine. The story also includes
     an account of the earthquake.

Secondary Sources

76   Chua, Chen Lok. "Two Chinese Versions of the American Dream:
     The Golden Mountain in Lin Yutang and Maxine Hong
     Kingston." *MELUS* 8:4 (Winter, 1981): 61-70.

77   Ling, Amy. *Between Worlds: Women Writers of Chinese
     Ancestry*. New York: Pergamon, 1990.
     A comprehensive historical and critical study of prose works
     by Chinese-American women writers, from the beginnings—e.g.,
     Sui Sin Far (Edith Eaton)—to the present—e.g., Maxine Hong
     Kingston and Amy Tan. Contains a bibliography with brief
     annotations.

78   ———. "Chinese American Women Writers: The Tradition
     Behind Maxine Hong Kingston." *Redefining American Literary
     History*. Eds. A. LaVonne Brown Ruoff and Jerry W. Ward, Jr.
     New York: MLA, 1990.
     Ling points out that a number of earlier Chinese women
     writing in the United States have been ignored and that Kingston
     did not spring out of nowhere, but is, rather, indebted to earlier
     women writers, such as Adet Anor, Meimei Lin, Helena Kuo,
     Jade Snow Wong, Janet Lim, Mai-Mai Sze, Han Suyin, Virginia
     Lee, Diana Chang, and Chuang Hua, some of whom wrote

autobiography and journalistic pieces or in Chinese rather than English or about experiences other than those having to do with being an immigrant or the descendant of immigrants.

CROATIAN (see also Slavic)

Individual Authors

79 Ifkovic, Edward. *Anna Marinkovich*. New York: Maryland Books, 1980.

At fourteen, Papa immigrated to a Croatian enclave in Milwaukee, doing grueling work in a factory; Mama at twelve immigrated alone. Together they go to Connecticut to buy cheap farmland, but the land turns out to be stony, and Papa must work in the quarries. Cut off from other Croatians and living in near poverty, the family experience one tragedy after another. Young and charming Joey rebels against his mother's rigid old-country values and refuses to work as his father does, but he gives in to alcoholism and depression. Younger Anna escapes the drudgery and grimness of the family through being an assiduous student.

80 Vecki, Victor G. *Threatening Shadows*. Boston: Stratford, 1931.

The only Croatian-American fiction written in English before World War II, it follows an immigrant doctor, Ivan Nemir, through a number of love affairs and his alienation from the Roman Catholic church until his final "true" love affair with Victoria, who saves him from cynicism.

Secondary Sources

81 Azulovic, Branimir. "Croatian-American Literature." *Ethnic Literatures Since 1776: The Many Voices of America*. Eds. Wolodymyr T. Zyla and Wendall M. Aycock. Lubbock: Proceedings of the Comparative Literature Symposium, Texas Tech University, Jan. 1976. IX (1978) I, 161-74.

A discussion of the three stages of Croatian-American literature: the peasant folktales and poems of the early immigrants; the development of the oral tradition, especially that concerning legendary Joe Magarac, the steelworker, between the world wars; and the writings of the highly educated post-World War II immigrants, mostly in Croatian. Azulovic explains that early prose writing in English was autobiographical, except for Vecki's novel, which he sees as largely unsuccessful.

CUBAN (see also Hispanic)

Individual Authors

82 Fernández, Roberto. *Raining Backwards*. Houston: Arte Publico, 1988.

Satiric exaggerations of episodes about a community of exiles from Castro's Cuba in Miami, who are waiting for the revolution which will allow them to return to their homeland. Through their own radio program and newspaper, they maintain a tightly knit community and keep in contact with those who have dispersed to the Midwest. The community is rife with family disintegration and madness: e.g., a young man believes that he is the pope, and a middle-aged woman seduces her errand boy and then accuses him of rape. But some do quite well financially, one by founding a plantain chip factory.

83 Garcia, Cristina. *Dreaming in Cuban*. New York: Knopf, 1992.

The story of three generations of Cuban women, some supportive of Castro's Cuba and some not. One of the daughters comes as a refugee to Brooklyn and opens the Yankee Doodle Bakery there, but her own daughter yearns to return to Cuba and especially to be reunited with her revolutionary grandmother in Havana.

84 Hijuelos, Oscar. *The Mambo Kings Play Songs of Love*. New York: Harper Perennial, 1991.

Two musician brothers—Cesar, a guitarist, and Nestor, a trumpeter—come from Cuba to New York in 1949 and become the core of a successful band. Nestor's son, Eugenio, tells the story of their close relationship despite their differences: Nestor, the quiet and stable brother, marries and dies young; Cesar lives the high party life, with one woman after another, and drinks himself to death at age sixty-one. For both, the highlight of their careers was appearing as guests on a popular television show which featured the famous Cuban entertainer, Desi Arnaz. A recent Hollywood film is based on this novel.

85 ———. *Our House in the Last World*. New York: Persea, 1983.

Alejo Santini comes to live in New York in 1939 with his wife Mercedes, hoping to have a better life there than he did on his dreary farm. Two sons are born—Horacio and Hector. In the 1950s, Alejo raises money to help the freedom fighters and is pleased when Castro is victorious, but his sister and her family in Cuba suffer under the new regime, and they come to New York aboard a "freedom flight." The older immigrants begin to resent the aid in employment and loans that are given to the new refugees, while they have had to struggle. After Alejo dies, Hector tries unsuccessfully to become more Americanized; but he is haunted by the ghost of his father and his recollections of stories about the old Cuba, and he remains tied to the Cuban community.

86 Muñoz, Elías Miguel. *Crazy Love*. Houston: Arte Publico, 1988.

An epistolary novel about an immigrant child coming of age and examining his family's past in Cuba and its present life in the United States.

87 ———. *The Greatest Performance*. Houston: Arte Publico, 1991.

An impressionistic novel told concurrently by Marito, who is gay, and his best friend, Rosita, a lesbian. As children in Cuba, they are best friends. Both immigrate as teenagers, with their families. Rosita, in California, learns to live the life of an independent American woman, with her own job, apartment, and lover, resisting the pressures of her family to marry. Marito, whose father continues to beat and scorn him for his effeminacy, drifts into various gay communities in New York and Miami. Some years later the two friends reconnect, but only in time for Rosita, as Marito's only true friend, to nurse him through his illness and death from AIDS.

88 Suárez, Virgil. *Welcome to the Oasis and Other Stories*. Houston: Arte Publico, 1991.

A novella and five stories which center on the lives of Cuban immigrants in the United States—their culture shock and linguistic confusion—as seen from the point of view of an immigrant from the Mariel boat lift in the 1960s.

89 Yglesias, José. *A Wake in Ybor City*. New York: Holt, Rinehart, and Winston, 1963.

In the 1950s the matriarch of a large extended family in the Cuban district of Tampa, where many of them have worked in the cigar factories, calls both her dispersed children and those who live nearby to a special family gathering. The gathering turns tragic when one of the grandchildren dies suddenly, and his wake becomes the occasion for an eruption of political differences among the family members: son Robert and son-in-law Esteban have been working secretly to supply the revolutionaries in Cuba, whereas daughter Elena, who managed to marry a rich Cuban in order to get out of Tampa's poverty, supports the established government of Battista. For other members of the family, tradition and the unity of the family supersede politics.

Anthologies

90 Hospital, Carolina, ed. *Cuban American Writers: Los Atrevidos*. Houston: Arte Publico, 1988.

An anthology of mainly poetry but some fiction by "the daring ones," the meaning of the sub-title, so named because they take the risk of writing in English though they are all Cuban born. In her introduction Hospital notes that these writers do not substitute one cultural heritage or literary tradition for another but rather blend both with the added sense of being exiles. Includes stories about the immigrant experience by Roberto Fernández, Elías Muñoz, and Pablo Medina, with introductions to the writers.

CZECH (see also Slavic)

Individual Authors

91 Auslander, Joseph and Audrey Wurdemann. *My Uncle Jan*. New York: Longmans, Green, 1948.

Connected stories from the point of view of a ten-year-old boy about his family, who immigrated from Bohemia to Wisconsin at the end of the nineteenth century. Uncle Jan, who came first with only twenty-five dollars in cash and has become the owner of acres of forest land, a saw mill, and a saloon, brings over the rest of the family and encourages other villagers to join him. In "New Bohemia" such agricultural festivals as *posviceni* and *obzinsky* and such religious festivals as the Feast of St. Wenceslas, patron saint of Bohemia, are joyously celebrated. Although Jan is busy, in American fashion, running his businesses, and Cousin Stefan, is involved in local politics, the women of the family ensure that good Bohemian food and customs are maintained.

92 Cather, Willa. *My Antonia*. New York: Houghton Mifflin, 1917.

An American man is the narrator of this story about his admiration, from youth to middle age, of the daughter of an immigrant from Bohemia to the Western prairies in the early part of the twentieth century. She manages her family's farm as a girl because her father, more an artist than a farmer, is unable to do so. Later, she works in town as a maid, and he notes that she retains the vigor and joy in life that she had earlier displayed, but which American-born young women seem to lack. Years later, returning from the East Coast, he finds her again, aging and still overworked, but he can still admire the vibrancy of her life, especially in contrast to his own life.

93 Chase, Mary Ellen. *Windswept*. New York: Macmillan, 1941.

For young adults. A novel which traces the experiences from the 1880s through the 1930s of the Marston family, Czech immigrants to Maine.

94 Jacobs, Emma Atkins. *A Chance to Belong*. New York: Dell, 1966.

For young adults. Jan Karel has difficulty pleasing both his immigrant parents in their desires for him to maintain their old country ways and himself in his desire to fit in with his high school friends. A new friend, Barbara, helps him to conciliate his parents while becoming the American that he is.

95 Krider, Ruby R. *Time and Tide*. Philadelphia: Dorrance, 1968.

A barely disguised autobiographical account. The author's mother experiences many hardships in raising three children on the prairies of Minnesota, Montana, and again Minnesota, because she married Frank Liska, a second generation man afflicted with American wanderlust and the inability to stick to anything. The child of fairly sophisticated immigrants from Prague, now hardworking farmers, and herself an immigrant at twelve, Emma Liska speaks to her children in detail of the geography, history, and legends told of Bohemia to her by her father. Her youngest daughter, the narrator, describes in detail the Czech immigrant society—the crafts, food, daily farm activities, manners and other behaviors—as well as the history of Montana and Minnesota—political and economic as well as social.

96 Ormonde, Czenzi. *Laughter from Downstairs.* New York: Farrar, Straus, 1948.

A collection of humorous stories from the point of view of nine-year-old Lida, growing up in an extended immigrant family in a town near Seattle. Her restaurant-owner father speaks eight languages and her mother speaks four, but neither speaks English without an accent, nor does she, for which she is called a foreigner at school. From her grandfather she learns Bohemian songs and legends, and from her grandmother how to make soup and dumplings. Her eccentric uncles and aunts include Ludmilla, who mails to them from North Dakota dried mushrooms packed in black stockings.

Secondary Sources

97 Machann, Clinton. "Hugo Chotek and Czech-American Fiction." *MELUS* 6:2 (Summer, 1979): 32-40.

A brief introduction to Czech-American fiction, most of it written in Czech. The focus is on Chotek's stories about immigrants in Texas, considered to be the high point of this literature, which was first published in a Czech journal out of Chicago, from 1880-1920.

98 Sturm, Rudolf. "Czech Literature in America." *Ethnic Literatures Since 1776: The Many Voices of America.* Eds. Wolodymyr T. Zyla and Wendall M. Aycock. Lubbock: Proceedings of the Comparative Literature Symposium, Texas Tech University, Jan. 1976. IX (1978): I, 161-72.

Claims that the poetry and non-fiction prose are superior to the fiction, which deals mainly with reminiscences of the old country, except for that of Egan Hostovsky, writer of three volumes of short stories and twenty novels, only a few of which, however, were written in English. Those written in Czech are concerned mainly with pre-World War II alienation and loneliness. After 1949, his English language works focus on political themes and espionage.

DANISH (see also Scandinavian)

Individual Authors

99 McDonald, Julie. *Amalie's Story.* New York: Simon and Schuster, 1970.
Amalie comes as an immigrant to Iowa in the late-nineteenth century and marries a man who becomes an important leader in their rural community.

100 Winther, Sophus Keith. *Mortgage Your Heart.* New York: Macmillan, 1937.
The sequel to *Take All to Nebraska.* Peter has become a citizen and is pleased that in Denmark he would be considered a rich man with his 320 acres of productive farmland, but his sons resent his authority and how hard he has always made them work. He also realizes that he must go into deep debt in order to own his farm and prevent another eviction. The sons have become almost thoroughly Americanized, whereas Martha, because of the farm woman's isolation, continues to speak only Danish. But even she, like her sons and husband, by the end, considers herself American, not Danish, and Nebraska as her home.

101 ———. *Take All to Nebraska.* New York: Macmillan, 1936. Reprint, Lincoln: University of Nebraska Press, 1976.
Peter and Martha Grimsen are too late, in the 1890s, to get free or cheap land in the Midwest, so they rent a farm near Springfield, Massachusetts. After having lost all their savings, they go to a Danish farming community in Nebraska, where they rent another. Their only daughter dies, and Peter drives his sons to work extra hard on the farm. Even so, after several years, they are evicted in favor of a buyer. Ready to give up and return to Denmark, Peter and Martha are befriended by a kinder American, who helps them find another farm to rent and restores some of their faith in the new land.

102 ———. *This Passion Never Dies.* New York: Macmillan, 1938.
The last novel in the trilogy, it focuses on Hans, who graduates from college and recalls his heritage with pride and his father, now, with respect.

Secondary Sources

103 Skårdal, Dorothy Burton. "A Danish Dream of America." *MELUS*
     8:4 (Winter, 1981): 5-23.
       A discussion of the fiction of the American experience in
     Danish, with a close look at the two novels of Enok Mortensen.
     Skårdal notes that, despite America's opportunities, Mortensen
     found it to be lacking in Danish graciousness. He wanted a dream
     that would "combine new-world spaciousness and individual
     freedom with old-world culture and sense of peoplehood."

DOMINICAN REPUBLIC (see also Hispanic)

Individual Authors

104 Alvarez, Julia. *How the Garcia Girls Lost Their Accent.* Chapel
     Hill, N.C.: Algonquin Books, 1991.
       Told in shifting time sequences, this is the story of the wealthy
     Garcia family, who are descendants of the conquistadors and live
     next to the palace of the dictator's daughter. When Dr. Carlos is
     discovered as having taken part in an unsuccessful coup, he flees
     with his wife, Laura, and their four daughters—Carla, Sandra,
     Yolanda and Sofia—to the Bronx. There the daughters become
     troublesome American teenagers and quickly forget their Spanish.
     Boarding school and counseling, in addition to the parents' old-
     country imposition of authority and the girls' remembering with
     nostalgia their grandparents' lessons—all serve to help them
     adjust more acceptably to American life.

DUTCH

Individual Authors

105 De Jong, David C. *Belly Fulla Straw.* New York: Knopf, 1934.
       Harmon Idema comes to Grand Rapids, Michigan to improve
     the chances for a good life for his children, but he is bitterly
     disappointed by the snobbishness of the earlier Dutch settlers and
     the narrowness of their religious views. He is further unhappy in
     his children's decisions to marry into that group and enjoy their
     society.

106 ————. *With a Dutch Accent.* New York: Harper and Brothers, 1944.

This autobiographical novel opens in a small seaside town in the Netherlands, where young David hears that America is a place of wilderness, adventure and quick riches. His father believes that he can improve his status and his family's future in Grand Rapids, Michigan, where there are many Dutch settlers. Once there, they are bitterly disappointed: they are cheated and oppressed by the earlier Dutch immigrants, whom they had counted on for help. Though an accomplished carpenter, the father can find work only as a menial laborer for a construction company, because he doesn't know American designs. The older sons must quit school to help support the family, but, eventually, David, the youngest, who has managed to stay in school with a part-time job, is able to go to college.

107 De Vries, Peter. *Blood of the Lamb.* Boston: Little, Brown, 1961.

Characterized by both hilarity and tragedy, this is the story of a young man growing up in a Dutch immigrant enclave on the south side of Chicago. His father had come merely on a visit to America, but stayed because he couldn't face the return sea voyage. The older son, a medical student and, to the consternation of his pious relatives, an atheist, dies suddenly, causing his brother to begin questioning the tenets of his Dutch Reformed faith. Marrying outside of his ethnic group also gives his parents grief. When his young daughter sickens and dies of leukemia, he completely loses faith in his family's values and their church.

108 Ferber, Edna. *So Big.* Garden City, N.Y.: Doubleday, Page, 1924. Reprint, Greenwich, CT: Fawcett, World, 1973.

Selina has spent most of her life traveling with her gambler father. When he dies, she gets a job in "High Prairie," Illinois, teaching the children of the hardworking and thrifty but narrow-minded Dutch immigrant farmers in the community. She marries one of them, Pervus DeJong, and despite the drudgery of her life, manages to keep up her high spirits. Her son Dirk becomes financially and socially successful, having chosen the safe profession of bookkeeper rather than the risky one of architect, and, seeming to have developed a personality fitting to the dour community in which he grew up, he is never able to be as carefree as his mother.

109 Gosselink, Sara. *Roofs Over Strawtown.* Grand Rapids, MI: Eerdman's, 1945.

A sentimental three-generation novel, with focus on the Vander Molen family. Janna and Gerhardt are members of a group of religious dissenters who leave the Netherlands in the mid-nineteenth century to build an isolated religious community in Iowa. Years later, in the town that has developed from its homesteading beginnings, their grandchildren are thoroughly American and know nothing of the hardships experienced by their ancestors. After Janna tells them the story, the youngsters take pride in their heritage.

110 Mulder, Arnold. *Bram of the Five Corners.* Chicago: McClurg, 1915.

Bram Meesterling leaves his farm and isolated southwest Michigan immigrant community to study at a nearby Dutch Reformed college and seminary in a nearby city. There, through the daughter of a settlement worker, he is exposed to shocking new values, particularly those from the new discipline of sociology. Whereas his parents believe that the fate of one's progeny must be left in the hands of God, Bram is persuaded that he must not marry his simple-minded fiancé. Breaking off his engagement, he is alienated from his home community.

111 ———. *The Dominie of Harlem.* Chicago: McClurg, 1913.

Freshly graduated from a seminary on the East Coast, the young "dominie" (Christian Reformed minister) Van Weelen, comes to serve a rural southwestern Michigan community founded by the followers of Van Raalte, who left the Netherlands in 1857 to escape the liberalism of the state church. The church members insist that only Dutch be spoken in their homes and at church and that their children be isolated from others, so that their religion and values will not be tainted. After the dominie's greatest antagonist, Jan Harmdyk, is exposed for his hypocrisy, Van Weelen's suggestions of English and picnics for the Sunday school children are looked upon more favorably.

112 ———. *The Outbound Road.* New York: Houghton Mifflin, 1919.

Bakkerzeel, a professor at a Dutch Christian college in southwestern Michigan, is ashamed to acknowledge his actress lover from Chicago and his illegitimate son, for whom he arranges adoption by a recent immigrant couple. The boy, always feeling out of place in the conservative community, goes to New York when he is grown, and Bakkerzeel deeply regrets his own hypocrisy and what he has missed as a result of it.

FILIPINO (see also Asian)

Individual Authors

113 Bulosan, Carlos. *America Is in the Heart.* 1946. Reprint, Seattle: University of Washington Press, 1973.

Although based on his own life, this narration represents the general experience of young Filipinos who came in the 1920s and 1930s to work in the U.S. Despite a miserable sea crossing, surviving sickness and death in the filthy hold of the ship, the narrator arrives in Seattle full of hope, but he and his fellow immigrants are tricked into virtual slave labor in a cannery in Alaska. In further episodes he moves about the West Coast, among other minorities, poor and looking for work, being exploited by employers, and becoming involved in violence.

114 ———. *If You Want to Know What We Are.* Minneapolis: West End, 1983.

Stories of young men in the Philippines, their reasons for emigrating, and their harsh experiences in the canning and fishing industries in California and the Northwest.

115 Hagedorn, Jessica Tarahata. *The Dogeaters.* New York: Pantheon, 1990.

Girls in the Philippines are so attuned to American culture, through the movies and popular music, that when one of them is sent to live in the United States, she experiences little popular culture shock, but after a time she finds that she feels truly at home in neither country.

116 ———. *Petfood and Tropical Apparitions.* San Francisco: Momo's, 1981.

Petfood is a bizarre novelette about gender switching and the California drug and entertainment scene. The young woman "George Sand" wants to be a writer. She comes from the

Philippines to California with her mother and her uncle "Aunt
Greta," and there she has many strange adventures.

117 Santos, Bienvenido. *Brothers, My Brothers*. Seattle: University of
Washington Press, 1979.
Stories of young men who came as students or laborers to the
United States and, cut off from their island homelands during
World War II and in the absence of Filipino women because of
immigration restrictions, are adrift in the United States, taking
odd jobs, drinking too much, playing endless games of poker, and
being pursued by blond women, who find them attractive but
whom they cannot marry because of anti-miscegenation laws.

118 ———. *The Man Who Looked Like Robert Taylor*. Seattle:
University of Washington Press, 1983.
More stories about immigrant males in the United States.

119 ———. *Scent of Apples*. Seattle: University of Washington Press,
1979.
Stories, again mostly about male immigrants, but contains
"Immigration Blues," about visiting Filipino women who come to
the U.S. on tourist visas seeking Filipino-American citizens to
marry.

120 ———. *You Lovely People*. Manila: Benipayo Press, 1965.
A collection of stories about young Filipinos in the 1940s,
whose expectations of American life have been destroyed and
who are lonely, wandering and lost. Ben, the narrator of the
stories, describes them as exiles who are unable to return home
and are suffering from discrimination, lacking Filipina consorts
and unhappy in relationships with American women, subsisting
on small wages from menial jobs, and fearing dying alone in a
country where they are unwelcome.

Anthologies

121 Cachapero, Emily, et al., eds. *Liwanag: Literary and Graphic
Expressions by Filipinos in America*. San Francisco: Liwanag,
1975.
"Liwanag" means brightness and understanding in Tagalog.
This collection contains graphics, photos, poetry, essays, and

some fiction—all chosen to depict a broad range of Filipino-American experiences, from many locales in the U.S. The introduction urges that immigrants and their children do not have to assimilate completely to the American mainstream in order to survive, but can acknowledge their heritage and still "function progressively" in this society. Fiction pieces are "Musings" and "The Believers" by Oscar Penaranda, and "I Came to Tell You Something" by Sam Tagatec.

FINNISH

Individual Authors

122 Miller, Helen. *Kirsti*. New York: Doubleday, 1964.

For young adults. Kirsti Junnola is the sixteen-year-old daughter of immigrants to Idaho. Trouble occurs when she wishes to marry a young man who is not Finnish.

123 Schoonover, Shirley. *Mountain of Winter*. New York: Coward-McCann, 1962.

Ava Knuutinen grows up with her immigrant grandmother, Mummu Korkiopaika, who has lost all her children in America—including two in World War II—in a rural Finnish community in a Northern state. Mel, forester for the state, comes to board with them and is introduced to all the Finnish customs still prevailing: e.g., the sauna, the music of the *kantele*, the midwinter festival of *laskianinen*, and the stories from the epic *Kalevala*. But, exposed as a thief and an abusive man, he runs off before he can be prosecuted. His temporary replacement, Paul, is initiated into the Finnish "manly arts" of drinking and fighting, passes those tests, and is something of a hero in fighting the fire that destroys half the community farms. Though Paul wishes to marry her, Ava will remain in the Finnish community and rebuild her burned farm.

Anthologies

124 Karni, Michael G. and Aili Jarvenpa. *Sampo, the Magic Mill*. Minneapolis: New Rivers, 1989.

Among poems and essays are some short stories about the immigrant experiences of Finns, mostly in northern Michigan,

Minnesota and the Northwest. Some stories written in Finnish are translated in a collection for the first time. Relevant stories, originally written in English, are Anna Perkkio, "Grandmother's Wedding Gift"; Lynn Maria Laitala, "Timo's Team"; Rebecca Cummings, "The Hair Brooch"; Ernest Hekkanen, "In the New World"; Eila Siren-Perlmutter, "Winter Trip" and "The Big Wedding"; Pierre Delattre, "Korrigan's Tree" and "The Spirit of the Water"; Lauri Anderson, "Hunting Hemingway's Trout"; Timo Koskinen, "Dead Weight"; and John Piirto, "Spur"; and an excerpt from Shirley Waisanen Schoonover's novel.

FRENCH

Individual Authors

125 Cather, Willa. *Death Comes for the Archbishop.* New York: Knopf, 1927.
A story about the life and death of a French priest in Santa Fe, New Mexico in the mid-nineteenth century.

126 Chopin, Kate. *The Complete Works of Kate Chopin.* Edited by Per Seyersted. Baton Rouge: Louisiana State University Press, 1969.
Contains a novel (*The Awakening.* Chicago: Herbert S. Stone, 1899), two previously published collections of stories (*Bayou Folk.* Boston: Houghton Mifflin, 1894 and *A Night in Acadie.* Chicago, 1897) and other stories, some unpublished, others published in magazines between 1891 and 1902, about the turn-of-the-century French community in Louisiana. Most of the settings are in Natchitoches Parish, and others are in and around New Orleans. The stories, which focus on women's struggles against their limited options, gained new attention from feminist scholars in the 1960s.

127 Erdman, Loula. *Room to Grow.* New York: Dodd, 1962.
For young adults. A novel about the Danton family who emigrate from France to the Texas Panhandle.

128 Hearn, Lafcadio [George W. Cable]. *Old Creole Days.* 1879. Reprint, Boston: Houghton Mifflin, 1943.
Romantic stories about the Creole society in New Orleans, set in the 1850s and 1860s.

129 ————. *Strange True Stories of Louisiana*. New York: Scribner's, 1889.

Realistic stories about the Creole society based on actual historical events which occurred between 1782 and the end of the nineteenth century.

130 Pundt, Helen. *Spring Comes First to the Willows*. New York: Crowell, 1963.

For young adults. Anna, the daughter of French immigrants, finds herself in conflict between her parents' culture and that of her schoolmates. Anna comes to reconcile both parts of her life and to be proud of her parents and her background.

FRENCH-CANADIAN

Individual Authors

131 Archambault, Alberic. *Mill Village*. Boston: Bruce Humphries, 1943.

A documentary novel about a family who come to Connecticut after the Civil War and experience the tedium and exploitation of work in the mills, the prejudice of the Yankees, and the new waves of immigrants from Canada after the 1900s.

132 Cormier, Robert. *Fade*. New York: Delacorte, 1988.

For young adults. In 1938 the Moreaux family move from Quebec to Massachusetts, settling in "Frenchtown," where the father has a job in a factory. Thirteen-year-old Paul inherits a special power (which has come to one boy in each of the family's generations) to "fade," that is to disappear, which enables him to see what others don't. When he grows up, although the power has gone, it has helped him to become a famous writer.

133 Ducharme, Jacques. *The Delusson Family*. New York: Funk and Wagnells, 1939.

Cecile and Jean-Baptiste come to a textile-mill town in Massachusetts in 1874 and raise six children. Hard work and the French church dominate their lives. The family remain closely knit, while the father becomes a successful carpenter and apartment building owner; a son and a daughter run a clothing shop; and one son becomes a priest. After Jean-Baptiste's death, Cecile and her oldest son fulfill their dream of owning a small farm.

134 Kerouac, Jack. *Doctor Sax: Faust, Part Three.* New York: Harcourt Brace, 1959.

Told in dream-like sequences, this is the story of a boy growing up in the "Little Canada" of Lowell, Massachusetts.

135 ———. *The Town and the City.* New York: Harcourt Brace, 1950. Reprint, 1978.

George and Marguerite Martin immigrate to a Massachusetts milltown and raise eight children there. Feeling too confined as well as like outsiders among the Yankees, the children move to New York City, where they continue to struggle with their sense of not belonging.

136 Metalious, Grace de Repentigny. *No Adam in Eden.* New York: Trident, 1967.

The Bergerons are an atypical French-Canadian immigrant family in a Massachusetts milltown, for whom the French community, its church, and its family values have no meaning. Armand dies of alcoholism; Monique is a cold, unloving woman who goes mad; and their daughter Angelique, after being rejected socially by the Yankee community, marries Etienne, but becomes an alcoholic and a social snob and has a series of affairs with Yankee professional men. Of their two daughters, Alana is cynical and unloving, but Leslie marries into and embraces a warm Italian-American family.

137 Plante, David. *The Francoeur Family.* London: Chatto and Windus, 1984.

A trilogy made up of *The Family,* 1978; *The Country,* 1981; and *The Woods,* 1982—all originally published by Gollancz—it is the story of three generations of a French immigrant family in Providence, Rhode Island. French is still spoken by and to the grandparents, but the rest keep apart from the French immigrant community.

138 Robichaud, Gérard. *Papa Martel.* New York: All Saints, 1961.

Louis and Cecile Martel immigrate to a New England milltown and raise their children bilingually and biculturally, adjusting to American life without losing their heritage or customs. One son becomes a priest, fulfilling the supposed dream of every French-Canadian family. Eventually, the parents move to Maine, but the family continue to be reunited at holidays and to preserve memories of their French-Canadian origins.

Secondary Sources

139 Chartier, Armand B. "The Franco-American Literature of New England: A Brief Overview." *Ethnic Literatures Since 1776: The Many Voices of America.* Eds. Wolodymyr T. Zyla and Wendall M. Aycock. Lubbock: Proceedings of the Comparative Literature Symposium, Texas Tech University, Jan. 1976. IX (1978) I, 193-215.

An introductory historical overview which points out that French-Canadian fiction in the U.S. illustrates an emphasis on family and church values as well as on the conflicts between assimilation and the attempts to preserve ethnic identity. The works of Jack Kerouac are the best expression of the "refusal to accept full cultural integration into the American mainstream."

140 ————. "Franco-American Literature: The New England Experience." *Ethnic Perspectives in American Literature: Selected Essays on the European Contribution.* Eds. Robert J. Di Pietro and Edward Ifkovic. New York: MLA, 1983.

Much like his earlier essay, this is an introductory summary of various genres; the section on the novel includes those written in French. The writers in English discussed briefly are Ducharme, Kerouac, Metalious, Robichaud, and Plante.

141 Sorrel, Richard S. "Novelists and Ethnicity: Jack Kerouac and Grace Metalious as Franco-Americans." *MELUS* 9:1 (Spring, 1982), 3-52.

The essay argues that those raised before World War II were shaped by their ethnicity, rather than that they shaped their own ethnicity. A bond exists between the two authors in that their backgrounds seem to be in conflict with their popular images.

GERMAN

Individual Authors

142 Bach, Marcus. *The Dream Gate.* Indianapolis: Bobbs, Merrill, 1949.

Hutterian immigrants founded this strictly patriarchal and reactionary Christian communist community in the Midwest, where its members could shun the world and live by true biblical rules and agricultural methods. In 1948, Joshua Volkner, who had run away at eighteen and is now a successful businessman in Chicago, comes to visit. He argues with the elders that there is more to life than work and prayer, that women have rights, and that men should defend their country. Listening to the Volkners describe the outside world, young Mike Neuman begins to question why he can't learn English, wear a watch, or go to the local county fair and ride on the Ferris wheel, why he cannot play music on the harmonica Joshua has secretly given him. The community gate becomes for him a symbol of a decision he must make between security and belonging and the adventure and opportunity that lie beyond it.

143 Baker, Betty. *The Dunderhead War.* New York: Harper and Row, 1967.

For young adults. Seventeen-year-old Quincy has some humorous adventures with his German-immigrant Uncle Fritz who volunteers to fight in the war against Mexico.

144 Benary-Isbert, Margot. *The Long Way Home.* Translated by Richard and Clara Winston. New York: Harcourt, Brace, 1959.

For young adults. Thirteen-year-old Christoph Wegener is a refugee from East Germany, who manages to get to the U.S. without his family. He bounces around from New York to Chicago to a ranch in California, trying to find a place where he can belong.

145 Derleth, August William. *Shadow of Night.* New York: Scribner's, 1943.

Hasso leaves the Tyrol in the 1840s to follow the man who killed his brother, finding him finally in Sac Prairie, Wisconsin.

But he has a change of heart because of the kindly people who live there.

146 Dreiser, Theodore. *Jennie Gerhardt*. New York: Harper and Brothers, 1911. Reprint, Cleveland: World, 1926, 1946.

Jennie, the oldest daughter of poor German immigrants in Ohio, is mistress to a U.S. senator who dies before he can marry her as he has promised, and then to Lester Kane, the wealthy son of successful Irish entrepreneurs. After giving birth to Kane's illegitimate daughter, she is disowned by her father and shunned by Kane's family. She is not hardened by her misfortune, however, as she later cares for her father in his old age and wishes Kane well in his marriage to a beautiful society woman.

147 Freitag, George H. *Lost Land*. New York: Coward-McCann, 1947.

A German community in Laurel, Massachusetts are divided in their national loyalties just prior to World War I. August Kreizer works in a mill until he can own his own farm, but the farm fails, and he and his family must return to town.

148 Hagedorn, Hermann. *The Hyphenated Family*. New York: Macmillan, 1960.

An autobiographical novel about growing up in New York City as a loyal German in the early part of the twentieth century. As the son of a successful businessman, Hermann often accompanies his parents on visits to Germany; but when they plan to return permanently, he remains to study at Harvard. When World War I begins, he realizes that he must choose American, not German patriotism, even though his family must then technically be the enemy. He experiences the pain of divided loyalties in wartime.

149 Hummel, George F. *Heritage*. New York: Stokes, 1935.

In 1846, railroad construction brings the first outsiders in 200 years to Norwalk, Connecticut, an inbred Yankee community: Mike McCarthy from Ireland, and Gottlob and Barbara Weller from Germany. Gottlob works as a laborer on John Beebe's farms, until he opens his own butcher shop in town. Barbara, a sophisticated woman, used to Stuttgart's cultural amenities, and the daughter of a friend of the philosopher Hegel, chafes under her treatment as a barbarian by the provincial Yankee women. However, the two eventually earn the townspeople's respect, and their two sons become extraordinarily successful Americans: one a wealthy merchant and the other the president of a prestigious New York university.

150   Jakes, John. *Homeland.* New York: Doubleday, 1993.

In 1857 Josef Kroner, son of a baker in a small town in southern Germany, immigrates to Cincinnati, changes his name to Joe Crown, and embraces his new country, emerging from the Civil War as a hero, and then establishing a successful brewery in Chicago. Nephew Paul, at age fourteen in 1892, comes to live with his uncle's family and learns to be a camera operator for the new moving pictures. Jakes sets the experiences of the immigrant (sailing from Hamburg in steerage, being processed at Ellis Island, finding temporary unskilled work in New York to earn the train fare to Chicago, learning to speak and understand English, being ridiculed as a greenhorn, retaining old country foods and customs, etc.) with the political and social events of the 1890s: the Chicago Exhibition, the development of the unions and the Pullman strike, and the Spanish American War. Historical figures such as Eugene Debs, Jane Addams, Teddy Roosevelt, and Stephen Crane are woven into the story.

151   Lion, Hortense. *The Grass Grows Green.* Boston: Houghton Mifflin, 1935.

Bavarian peasants Bertholde and Hana Willmarck send their youngest children to the United States in 1852 to join their two older brothers, because in Germany their future is threatened by war and military conscription. They settle in a German community in New York. Frieda marries a businessman, and the two of them remain notedly pacifist; but Siegfried wishes to fight for his new country and is killed in the Civil War. As an old woman, Frieda learns with great sadness that her grandsons are volunteering to fight against Germany in World War I.

152   Pine, Hester. *The Waltz Is Over.* New York: Farrar and Reinhart, 1943.

A three-generation novel about a family who immigrated from Ulm in 1845. The Multschers found a brewery in the U.S. The parents retain their culture, but the children become Americanized.

153 Richter, Conrad. *The Free Man.* New York: Knopf, 1943.

For young adults. In the eighteenth century, a young indentured servant crosses the ocean on a rickety ship, undergoes hunger, cruelty from the crew, and dangerous ocean storms. Once in Philadelphia, he learns that he has been cheated of his possessions and that he faces exploitation as a bond servant as well as contempt for being German. Escaping from his cruel master and his scornful daughter, he joins a backwoods settlement across the mountains, eventually becoming an officer and hero in the colonial army. After their victory, he marries the daughter of his former English master, now in disgrace for having been a loyalist.

154 Saltzman, Eleanor. *Ever Tomorrow.* New York: Coward-McCann, 1936.

A three-generation novel about German-American farmers in Iowa. Joe Mueller puts all of his hopes into his farm.

155 Singmaster, Elsie. *I Heard of a River: A Story of the Pennsylvania Germans.* New York: Holt, 1948.

For young adults. Hannes escapes persecution in Germany and joins a band of Swiss Mennonites, going with them to William Penn's colony in the United States. There they will live in a new settlement on the Susquehanna River.

156 ———. *The Magic Mirror.* Boston: Houghton Mifflin, 1934.

For young adults. Jesse Hummer, the child of immigrants in Allentown, Pennsylvania, 1900, wants to be a writer, but his family's financial position make it impossible for him to go to college. Taking a cue from old masters, he decides to write anyway, about what he knows.

157 Suckow, Ruth. *Country People.* New York: Knopf, 1924.

The story of the Kaetterhenrys and the Baumgartners, who came to the Iowa frontier from Germany in the 1840s. Through their industry and the retention of their old country values bykeeping apart from the other settlers, they leave prosperous farms to their descendants, when others fail to do so.

158 Williamson, Joanne S. *And Forever Free*. New York: Knopf, 1966.

 For young adults. Martin, a sixteen-year-old orphan, comes to live with his uncle in New York in the 1860s, just prior to the Civil War. The problems of adjusting to the culture and the temper of the times are well illustrated in the story.

Secondary Sources

159 Arndt, Karl J. *Early German American Narratives*. New York: American Books, 1941.

 The introductory essay is a survey and explanation of the very extensive amount of immigrant literature written in German in nineteenth-century America. Only three narratives in English are included: one about life in Texas in the 1850s by Charles Sealsfield (Karl Postl); and two by Friedrich Gerstacker about life in Mississippi and among the Pennsylvania Germans.

160 Bishoff, Robert. "German-American Literature." *Ethnic Perspectives in American Literature: Selected Essays on the European Contribution*. Eds. Robert J. Di Pietro and Edward Ifkovic. New York: MLA, 1983.

 A historical survey of works in both German and English, beginning with the literary movements in three main geographical areas: Pennsylvania, Texas, and the Midwest. It suggests that in the eighteenth and nineteenth centuries German-American literature in English was closely parallel to the literature of the nation as a whole and therefore not much preoccupied with the immigrant experience. Bishoff lists, with few comments, a number of twentieth century writers of German background, who did not use the immigrant experience as the basis for their fiction.

161 Condoyannis, George. *Journal of German American Studies*. Vol. 4 (1972).

 Contains thirty-eight synopses of novels, written between 1850 and 1918, many about the immigrant experience, but all in German: a "grossly neglected area of German-American literary history." Most of the fiction about the immigrant experience was written in German and has never been translated into English.

162 Tolzmann, Don Heinrich, compiler. *German-Americana: A Bibliography.* Metuchen, NJ: Scarecrow, 1975.

    A collection of essays on German-American poets, journalists, historians, dramatists and novelists—but only those who wrote in German. Tolzmann points to the great amount of fiction about the German-American immigrant experience that has not been translated.

GERMANS FROM RUSSIA

Individual Authors

163 Breneman, Mary Worthy, pseud. [Mary Worthy Thurston and Muriel Breneman.] *The Land They Possessed.* New York: Macmillan, 1956.

    A New England family make a number of moves to new territories in the West to satisfy the desires of the ambitious father. In one of their settlements in the Dakotas, from 1885-1894, the daughter overcomes the Yankee prejudices against the growing body of new German-Russian immigrant farmers in the area and marries one of them rather than move farther west with her family.

164 Lindsay, Mela Meisner. *Shukar Balan: The White Lamb.* Lincoln, NE: American Historical Society of Germans from Russia, Augustums, 1976.

    This novel, based on the lives of the author's parents, begins with an explanation of how German farmers were sent by their government to settle in the Volga region of Russia and traces one family's history in immigrating to Kansas when Germans began to be persecuted in Russia in the early part of the twentieth century. There are detailed accounts of the train trip to Hamburg, the processing by the ship's company, the unhealthy conditions aboard ship, the processing at Ellis Island, and the train trip to Kansas. There, they work assiduously on a rented farm but are taunted by the earlier settlers, first as Russians and then, during World War I, as Germans. Eventually, continuing hard work and integrity bring them respect and some prosperity.

165 Sykes, Hope Williams. *The Joppa Door.* New York: Putnam's, 1937.

A woman follows her minister husband to Utah and is bitterly disappointed by her experiences: seasickness and filth on the ship, baggage stolen at the railroad terminal, and her husband's expulsion from the church because of his refusal to be polygamous. They become tenant farmers.

166 ———. *The Second Hoeing.* New York: Putnam's, 1935.

A tyrant immigrant father keeps his children hard at work on their Colorado beet farm, refusing to allow them to go to school or otherwise assimilate into American society.

GREEK

Individual Authors

167 Brelis, Dean. *My New Found Land.* Boston: Houghton Mifflin, 1963.

Young Dimitri Chrysofilos is the nephew of Stavros, one of the first Greek immigrants in Newport, Rhode Island, who entertains the Yankee fishermen with stories about the Aegean and with homemade wine. While in public school with children of many ethnic groups, Dimitri tries to be a good Greek: he helps the priest at the Orthodox church, Father George, who knows no English, and he operates, with the help of the Black Bob Buchanan, a small shoe repair shop, to help support his family when his father is sick. But he also wants to be a good American and does not accept his mother's desire to bring a nice girl from Greece to be his wife.

168 Cotsakis, Roxanne. *The Wing and the Thorn.* Atlanta: Tupper and Lane, 1952.

John Pantellis leaves his rural home near Kalamata, hoping to make his fortune in America and return, but after many years pass, his grown children are annoyed with his retention of his "Greekness," considering themselves to be American. John returns to Greece but finds that it is not the same place that he left and that he can no longer consider it his home.

169 Demetrios, George. *When Greek Meets Greek.* Boston: Houghton Mifflin, 1947.

Twenty-five humorous short pieces, some like fables, some

anecdotal, about Greeks in Greece and as immigrants in the United States, mostly in Boston, some in Kansas City .

170   Dilles, Jim. *The Good Thief.* New York: Thomas Crowell, 1959.

A humorous and touching story about family love and community solidarity. Costas Desmas is on strike in a packing house in California and cannot support his wife Thespina and their four children. He and his friend Pericles alternately picket and drink wine, recollecting stories about their days in Greece. After Costas's young son and his friends steal a steer and it is discovered by the police, Costas is taken to jail; but while there he becomes the hero of a newspaper story about the plight of the packing house workers, and, when the strike ends, he gets his old job back.

171   Jarvis, Charles E. *The Tyrants.* Lowell, MA: Ithaca Press, 1972.

During the depression, when the textile mills are idle and poverty is widespread, Peisistratus Zacharias, owner of a coffeehouse in "Cabot City," Massachusetts, wants to gain the kind of political power for the Greek community that the Irish and the French-Canadians have. He must also deal with the local bishop, who is responsible for a conflict over religious politics among the members of the Greek church. Roosevelt wins the 1932 election, a new priest comes to help unify the church members, and Zacharias forms the Diogenes Democratic Club, a budding political machine.

172   ———. *Zeus Has Two Urns.* Lowell, MA: Apollo Books, 1976.

A companion in time and setting to *Tyrants*, but the perspective is from twelve-year-old Socrates Genos and focuses on his street adventures when he isn't attending the Greek parochial school or working at his father's small restaurant, which eventually is closed because it is not self-supporting. Socrates notices such things as bootleg whiskey and the payoff of the Irish cops, as well as the establishment of a Greek political club and a campaign speech by Franklin Roosevelt. The father's subsequent illness and death leave Socrates as the male mainstay of the family.

173   Kazan, Elia. *America, America.* New York: Stein and Day, 1962.

When the Turks are persecuting the Greeks and Armenians in

Macedonia, young Stavros Topouzoglou is sent by his family to Constantinople with all their treasures to make way for their resettlement, but on the way he is robbed and then, working as a laborer in the city, is cheated. Eventually he is befriended by a rich American woman who helps arrange his passage to the U.S., but, accused by her husband aboard ship as a trouble-maker, he is to be deported. His consumptive friend Hohanness gives Stavros his identification papers, and Stavros jumps ship and swims to shore from Ellis Island. In New York, he assumes the name Joe Arness, sends his parents what money he has, and, as a shoeshine boy, will work to bring them to America.

174   ———. *The Anatolian.* New York: Knopf, 1982.
A sequel to *America, America.* Stavros has earned enough money working for a carpet dealer to send for his parents and brothers and sisters. His father, however, has died suddenly before sailing, and Stavros must become the head of the family and provide for the rest of them, which he does in so autocratic a way that they all resent him. Stavros eventually becomes successful enough in business that he can invest in a scheme to help his native Anatolia and become a hero in the eyes of his dead father's ghost.

175   Mountzoures, H. L. *The Bridge.* New York: Scribner's, 1972.
Immigrant Christos Neros returns to Epirus to marry Thalia, and they come together to settle on the coast in Connecticut, producing eight children. Christos' infidelity and other abuses help to bring about Thalia's insanity, and the children are shuffled periodically to unloving foster homes. At twenty-six, Philip, the oldest child visits Greece and tells his cousin that Greek immigrants in America are spiritually doomed, that immigration is a mistake, but, after a serious illness, he returns to Connecticut and "bridges" the gap with his father.

176   ———. *The Empire of Things and Other Stories.* New York: Scribner's, 1968.
Among other stories are these about Greek immigrants on the East Coast: "The Beating," "The Buoy," "Love and Wisdom," "Fathers," "A Lecture," and "A Reunion."

177 Petrakis, Harry. *Days of Vengeance*. New York: Doubleday, 1983.

The story of the interconnected destinies of three men who emigrate separately from Crete in 1909. Stellios Trombakis murders a young man whom he envies and runs away, ending up in a railroad gang in Utah. A rough and unethical man, he is reformed through both violence and kindness, to become a union organizer for the miners. Manolis, the brother of the murdered man, follows Stellios to the U.S. to get revenge. Father Basil takes his wife and three children to minister to the Greek mining community in Utah. There the three men's lives become intertwined as they battle together the injustices of the mine owners.

178 ———. *A Dream of Kings*. New York: David McKay, 1966.

Leonidas Matsoukas fought for Greece in World War II, then came to Chicago and opened the Pindar Counseling Service, giving advice on love, real estate investment, bedwetting and other problems. Discovered to be cheating at cards, he is severely beaten by the Turk Youssouf, who spares his life when he pleads that he has been hoping to make enough money to take his sick son Stavros back to Greece for a cure. Though his wife Calliope holds him in contempt for his economic failures and his affair with the lusty widow Anthoula, she takes pity on him and gives him her life savings so that he and the dying boy may go to Greece.

179 ———. *Ghost of the Sun*. New York: St. Martin's, 1990.

A sequel to *A Dream of Kings*. Matsoukas' son has died in Greece, and Matsoukas is imprisoned and tortured by the new government for supposed political crimes. After an eight-year absence, he returns to Chicago, finding that his wife has remarried a very wealthy businessman, Sophocles Gravoulis, who admires Matsoukas as a great hero and offers him both social and financial help; and his wife and daughters welcome him home enthusiastically and without reproaches. But Matsoukas, uneasy in the wealthy Greek community and as the ex-husband of a wife he still loves, chooses to take care of a young unmarried woman and her son and to track down his old enemy, the Turk Youssouf. But finding him paralyzed and in a nursing home, Matsoukas, instead, befriends and cares for him, and searches for his newer enemy, Farmakis, who had tortured and crippled him in the Greek prison, before escaping to Chicago when the dictator's regime was overthrown.

180 ———. *Lion at My Heart*. Boston: Little, Brown, 1959.

The widower Angelo Varinakis and his son Mike, a World War II veteran, work in the steel mills in South Chicago. Mike's marrying an Irish woman causes a rift with his father, who wants to preserve the family's Greek culture. Younger brother and college student Tony pleases his father by marrying a Greek woman, but when Angelo refuses to be reconciled with Mike, the priest Father Kontoyannis shames Angelo by pointing out his hypocrisy, for having had an adulterous affair with a non-Greek woman.

181 ———. *Nick the Greek*. New York: Doubleday, 1979.

A fictionalized account of the life of Nicholas Andrea Dandelos, who came to Chicago from Crete in 1919, with $25,000 lent to him by his godfather to start a business. After losing the money by gambling, he is tutored on the art by old Nestor, makes a fortune gambling with Chicago and New York mobsters, gives millions to charity, and dies bankrupt in Las Vegas in 1966 at the age of eighty-four.

182 ———. *The Odyssey of Kostas Valakis*. New York: David McKay, 1963.

The illiterate son of a herdsman, Kostas marries Katerina for her dowry, and they come to Chicago. There they both work long shifts in Glavros' restaurant in order to become restaurant owners themselves, the better to provide for their children. But after the oldest son Aeneas dies as a child, and Alexander kills his brother Manuel and goes to prison, Kostas realizes that his dream of a better life in America has become a nightmare.

183 ———. *Pericles on 31st Street*. Chicago: Quadrangle, Books, 1965.

Stories of Greek immigrants in a Greek enclave in Chicago, their pride in and adherence to their culture and traditions. The title story, "The Wooing of Ariadne," "The Miracle," "The Legacy of Leontis," "Pa and the Sad Turkeys," "Courtship of the Blue Widow," and "Matsoukas" are particularly recommended.

184 ———. *The Waves of Night and Other Stories*. New York: David McKay, 1969.

A later collection of stories, similar to those in *Pericles on 31st Street*.

185 Vardoulakis, Mary. *Gold in the Streets*. New York: Dodd, Mead, 1945.

George Vardas and his two friends are recruited in Crete to work in the cloth mills in Chicopee, Massachusetts. Appalled by their reception at Ellis Island and with the factory town, they intend to stay only temporarily. But, despite hostility from the earlier Polish immigrants working at the mills, two of them decide instead to stay permanently, sending for other family members and their local priest and his daughter, whom George Vardas has long wanted to marry. Michali opens his own coffee house, as the Greek community grows and flourishes. Petros, however, returns to his family in Greece with his savings to pay for his ailing son's operation.

Secondary Sources

186 Karanikas, Alexander. "Greek-American Literature." *Ethnic Perspectives in American Literature*. Eds. Robert J. Di Pietro and Edward Ifkovic. New York: MLA, 1983.

An introductory historical survey of prose and poetry, with a summary of themes in immigrant fiction, comments on individual writers, and a bibliographical note.

187 ———. *Hellenes and Hellions: Modern Greek Characters in American Literature, 1825-1975*. Urbana: University of Illinois Press, 1981.

A comprehensive historical and critical survey of Greeks as characters in fiction as well as of Greek-American writers, with a discussion of the themes common to immigrant fiction: e.g., the social conditions in the old world, the conflicts in family relationships, the response of neighbors, alienation, the pull between ethnicity and Americanization, the nostalgia for what has been lost, and the desire for improved social status. The most useful chapters are 3, "The Greek as Immigrant"; 5, "Growing Up Greek"; and 11, "The Greeks of Petrakis."

HISPANIC (see also Cuban, Dominican, Mexican, Puerto Rican, and Salvadoran)

Anthologies

188   Alegría, Fernando and Jorge Ruffinelli, eds. *Paradise Lost or Gained: The Literature of Hispanic Exile.* Houston: Arte Publico, 1991.

   Stories by and about Cuban, Mexican, and Puerto Rican immigrants in "exile" from their native lands.

189   Augenbraum, Harold and Ilan Stavans. *Growing Up Latino: Memoirs and Stories.* Boston: Houghton Mifflin, 1993.

   The editors explain that Latinos (or Hispanics) have as traditional commonality the Spanish language, the Roman Catholic religion (mixed with various native shamans), and "political disaffection from the Anglo and ruling class." The five groups they distinguish are Mexicans, Cubans, Central Americans, Puerto Ricans, and Caribbeans (basically Dominicans). The twenty-five selections (most of them fiction and Mexican, with a few Cuban and Puerto Rican, and one by the Dominican Julie Alvarez) were chosen on the bases of their having been written by genuine Hispanics, of being about growing up, and of possessing "powerful prose." There are three thematic divisions: "Imagining the Family" (about domestic matters), "Gringolandia" (about coping in Anglo territory), and "Songs of Self Discovery" (about finding one's own identity).

190   Kanellos, Nicolás, ed. *Short Fiction by Hispanic Writers of the United States.* Houston: Arte Publico, 1991.

   Twenty-one stories: four Cuban, fourteen Mexican, and three Puerto Rican, written originally in English about the American experience, the authors having been published by Arte Publico Press. The book includes an introductory, historical essay and brief introductions to the writers by the editor.

191   Kanellos, Nicolás, and Luis Davila, eds. *Latino Short Fiction.* Special Issue of *Revista Chicano-Riquena* 8, 1 (Winter, 1980).

   Prize winning stories by Chicanos, Puerto Ricans, Colombians, Peruvians, Cubans, and Chileans living in the United States.

192 Keller, Gary D. and Francisco Jiménez, eds. *Hispanics in the United States: An Anthology of Creative Literature.* Ypsilanti, MI: Bilingual Review Press, 1980.
A collection of poetry, drama, and fiction.

193 Poey, Delia, and Virgil Suarez. *Iguana Dreams: New Latino Fiction.* New York: Harper Perennial, 1992.
A collection of thirty stories by now recognized writers, most of them Mexican-, Cuban-, and Puerto Rican Americans, but includes one Chilean- and one Dominican-American. The editors, Mexican- and Cuban-American, respectively, note what the writers share—bilingualism and the need for cultural survival—and how they are different: e.g., the rural versus the urban traditions—the barrios of the Southwest or Chicago of the Mexicans versus those of New York for the Puerto Ricans; the ties to the land of the Mexicans versus the ties to water of the Cubans and Puerto Ricans; and the varieties of Roman Catholic practices.

194 Vigil-Piñon, Evangelina, ed. *Woman of Her Word: Hispanic Women Write.* Houston: Arte Publico, 1987.
Among forty pieces of poetry, critical studies, and fiction by Cuban, Mexican, and Puerto Rican writers are immigrant stories by Sandra Cisneros and Nicholasa Mohr. The critical introduction is by the editor.

Secondary Sources

195 Horno-Delgado, Asunción, Eliana Ortega, Nina M. Scott, and Nancy Saporta Sternbach, eds. *Latina Writing and Critical Readings.* Amherst: University of Massachusetts Press, 1989.
Although this collection includes mostly works in Spanish, especially poetry, by women of Cuban, Mexican, and Puerto Rican backgrounds, it also contains essays on and by some writers of English fiction. Includes a bibliography of primary and secondary works compiled by Elaine N. Miller and Nancy Saporta Sternbach.

196 Kanellos, Nicolás. *A Biographical Dictionary of Hispanic Literature in the United States: The Literature of Puerto Ricans,*

Cuban Americans, and Other Hispanic Writers. New York: Greenwood, 1989.
   An introduction to writers and their works. Contains a bibliography and index.

HUNGARIAN

Individual Authors

197 Lewiton, Mina. *Elizabeth and the Young Stranger.* Eau Claire, WI: Hale, 1961.
   For young adults. A Hungarian refugee girl tries to make friends with her schoolmates, but meets resentment, largely from their parents.

198 Stibran, Teréz. *The Streets Are Not Paved with Gold.* Cleveland: published by the author, 1961.
   Stephen Strohm's parents come to Cleveland at the turn of the century; his father works as a laborer and his mother takes in boarders, until they are able to open a small grocery store, buy a small farm, and send Stephen to medical school. Terry Marianivsky leaves her village in 1920, when it becomes part of Czechoslovakia and meets Stephen in Cleveland. A skilled seamstress, Terry is exploited by her employers; and still strongly connected to her family, she returns to Europe. But the changes in her home and her sense of better opportunities in the U.S. as well as her love for Stephen bring her back, and she eventually becomes a buyer for a suburban department store.

Secondary Sources

199 Basa, Enikö Molnár. "Hungarian-American Literature." *Ethnic Perspectives in American Literature: Selected Essays on the European Contribution.* Eds. Robert J. Di Pietro and Edward Ifkovic. New York: MLA, 1983.
   A historical and critical survey of the three periods of Hungarian immigration and their resultant literatures: all but Stibran's novel are written in Hungarian.

200 Gellén, Jósef. "Acceptance and Rejection: Proto-Ethnicity in

Some Hungarian-American Writings." *MELUS* 12:4 (Winter, 1985), 25-35.

A discussion of the trilogies of two different authors, writing in Hungarian, who expressed a different kind of ethnicity from what it now means. In these novels the immigrants reject most of what the U.S. stands for and do not want to assimilate.

201 Konnyu, Leslie. *A History of American Hungarian Literature: Presentation of American Authors of the Last Hundred Years and Selections from their Writings*. St. Louis: Cooperative of American Hungarian Writers, 1962.

An extensive survey of the literature, almost all of it written in Hungarian and very little of it translated into English.

INDIAN (see also Asian)

Individual Authors

202 Mukherjee, Bharati. *Darkness*. Toronto: Penguin, 1985. Reprint, New York: Ballantine Books, 1992.

Twelve short stories, mostly about Indian immigrants in Iowa, Georgia, California, and New York. Particularly recommended for views of immigrant life are "Angela," "A Father," "Nostalgia," "Visitors," and "The Imaginary Assassin."

203 ————. *Jasmine*. New York: Grove, 1989. Reprint, New York: Ballantine Books, 1991.

Jyoti, widowed by a terrorist bomb, flies from India through Europe on unchartered planes and enters the Florida coast illegally by boat. Undergoing a brutal rape, after which she kills her attacker, she is taken in by Lillian Gordon, who runs a camp to help illegal immigrant women from Central America. She is coached on American behavior and sent to New York. After a brief stay in an Indian enclave in Queens, she becomes Jasmine, a nanny in Manhattan. Believing that she is being followed by her husband's murderer, she flees to a small Iowa town, and, as Jane, lives with Bud Ripplemeyer. The two adopt Du, a Vietnamese orphan. For different reasons, both Du and Jane leave for California, which they hope is their last refuge. As hardy survivors, they represent the new breed of Americans who will give new life to the country.

204 ———. *The Middleman and Other Stories*. New York: Grove Press, 1988. Reprint, New York: Ballantine Books.

Stories of Indian and West Indian immigrants making their way in New York, Toronto, Iowa, and Michigan. Particularly recommended are the title story, "A Wife's Story," "The Tenant," "Jasmine," and "The Management of Grief."

205 ———. *The Tiger's Daughter*. Boston: Houghton Mifflin, 1971.

Tata, the daughter of a wealthy businessman in Calcutta, goes to Vassar College and initially experiences the culture shock of an Asian among American students. She marries an American and comes to feel so at home in her new country that when she returns to visit her parents in India she finds the Indian society and political climate dismaying, and she is anxious to return to the United States.

206 ———. *Wife*. New York: Houghton Mifflin, 1975. Reprint, New York: Ballantine Books, 1992.

In Calcutta, Dimple Dasgupta chooses not to take her university exams in favor of idleness at her parents' house and waiting for a romantic movie-style life as the wife of a neurosurgeon. But the best her father can get her is an engineer, Amit Basu. The couple immigrate to New York and live among a circle of other Indian engineers and their wives. Believing that they will return to India with plentiful savings, most of the women consort only with other Indians and retain their dress and their customs. But Dimple meets some assimilated, independent Indian women, who urge her to imitate them. Afraid of them as well as of going out alone and dealing with merchants, Dimple has a serious mental breakdown.

IRANIAN

Individual Authors

207 Rachlin, Nahid. *Foreigner*. New York: Norton, 1978.

When she is eighteen, the daughter of a shopkeeper in Teheran comes to study at a college in Boston, eventually earning a graduate degree in biology and marrying a college professor. Fourteen years later she returns to Iran to visit her father, and unexpectedly, her mother, who had supposedly deserted her when she was a child. Because she has become almost thoroughly Americanized, she is repelled at first to be in the midst of what she now believes is a backward and sexist culture. But it is not long before she realizes that American life, with its pressures to earn money and to succeed, does not offer the spiritual and emotional fulfillment that she feels in a small Iranian city with her mother and a doctor who has studied in the U.S. but returned to Iran to practice medicine. She refuses to accompany her husband back to the U.S. when he comes to fetch her.

208 ———. *Married to a Stranger*. New York: Dutton, 1983.

Minou, the daughter of a lawyer, grows up in Ahvaz during the reign of the Shah, when he is trying to modernize the country. She finds her life too restrictive and boring and longs to go to America, where her brother Sohrab is a student at the University of Wisconsin. But her father won't allow it. She marries her high school teacher, Javad Partovi, who is attacked by the city's conservatives for his liberal columns in the newspaper and also for his adultery. Javad gives Minou some of her dowry money and a letter of permission to leave the country. She goes to Boston University, where finally she feels free and in charge of her life.

IRISH

Individual Authors

209 Beckley, Zoe. *A Chance to Live*. New York: Macmillan, 1918.

Thirteen-year-old Annie Hargan must quit school in New York in the 1890s to support her widowed mother and younger siblings. An employee in a shirtwaist sweatshop, she survives the fire that kills over a hundred other women employees. She comes to realize that women, as much as men, are exploited and endangered by the labor system, and none more than recent immigrants, the Jewish and Italian newcomers, who must return to work under the same conditions that caused the fire because they do not have her advantages of being American born and, as an Irish-American, a knowledge of English.

210 Cleary, James Mansfield, ed. *The Nebraska of Kate McPhelim Cleary*. Lake Bluff, IL: United Educators, 1958.

A selection of stories about Irish immigrants in rural settlements in Nebraska.

211   Curran, Mary Doyle. *The Parish and the Hill.* Boston: Houghton Mifflin, 1948. Reprint, Stony Brook, N.Y.: Feminist Press, 1986.
      In Holyoke, Massachusetts, a daughter of the immigrant O'Sullivan family, mill workers, marries ambitious James O'Connor, who moves out of the shanties of the Irish parish and onto the outskirts of the hill, where the "lace-curtain" Irish try to assimilate with the English. When the mills close during the depression, the O'Connors must move back to the parish, with whose members daughter Mary, the narrator, has never ceased to be in sympathy.

212   Deasy, Mary. *The Hour of Spring.* Boston: Little, Brown, 1948. Reprint, New York: Arno Press, 1976.
      A three-generation family chronicle narrated by Bridget, the granddaughter of Matt Joyce, who came to the U.S. from County Kerry in 1870. Bridget interviews three aging family members, who tell of their lives in Ireland and their immigration to the United States. A younger cousin describes the Easter Uprising of 1916. The story ends with the death of Cousin Timothy in 1926.

213   Dineen, Joseph. *Queen Midas.* Boston: Little, Brown, 1958.
      A straightforward story about Pegeen Dooley, who, at age thirteen, is given passage money from Dublin to "Boyleston" (Boston) to live with her immigrant aunt. She works in a factory until she is eighteen, then marries Patrick O'Connell. Through her skill at money management and investments, she becomes extremely wealthy and a powerful political force in the city, setting up illustrious careers for her three sons in politics, journalism, and business.

214   ———. *Ward Eight.* 1936. Reprint, New York: Arno Press, 1976.
      Dennis O'Flaherty immigrates to Boston and meets Hughie Donnelly, a ward boss who gets jobs and tenement flats for new immigrants in exchange for political loyalty. Dennis's son Tim succeeds Donnelly and becomes an important political figure in the Irish middle class.

215   Driscoll, Charles B. *Kansas Irish.* New York: Macmillan, 1943.

"Big Flurry," Florence Driscoll, a West Cork fisherman, born in 1836, comes to Kansas and has seven children. By the time his children are grown, he is sick of farm life and misses Ireland. His wife and children give him the money to return to Ireland.

216 Dunphy, Jack. *Jack Fury: A Novel in Four Parts*. 1946. Reprint, New York: Arno Press, 1976.

An immigrant coal-wagon driver in Philadelphia loses his wife and must raise his children alone. He remarries, to Bridget, a servant girl. His son turns against him, his two daughters make bad marriages, and he loses his job at age fifty-four because trucks are replacing horse-drawn carriages.

217 ———. *The Murderous McLaughlins*. New York: McGraw-Hill, 1988.

Immigrant and matriarch Mary Ellen McClaughlin gives her grandson a sense of Irish identity in Philadelphia in the 1920s; his father and uncle are weak and have lost theirs.

218 Egan, Maurice Francis. *The Disappearance of John Longworthy*. 1890. Reprint, New York: Arno Press, 1977.

In New York in the 1880s, the four O'Connor children live a dreary life in a two-room apartment in the Bowery because of a brutal drunk of a father. Daughter Rose is killed when Mrs. O'Connor throws an iron at Mr. O'Connor and misses. In contrast, the middle-class Galligan family live in a comfortable precinct on the East Side, keeping themselves apart from the Irish lower class and disapproving of the new immigrants from Southern and Eastern Europe. And Nellie Mulligan rises from the servant and laborer class by taking a position as a shopgirl, imitates middle class manners, and organizes a shopgirls' social club.

219 Farrell, James T. *Studs Lonigan: A Trilogy*. New York: Vanguard, 1935.

The three books were originally published separately as *Young Lonigan: A Boyhood in Chicago Streets* (1932), *The Young Manhood of Studs Lonigan* (1934), and *Judgment Day* (1935), all by Vanguard. Studs' grandfather was an immigrant laborer, a pauper and a drunk. Studs' father, Patrick, the only successful child, a businessman, moves his family into a middle-class neighborhood in Chicago, where he can have distance from his

Irishness and the power of the Church. However, Studs rebels against his parents' values, joins a street gang while in the eighth grade, and goes on to live a life of violence and drunkenness, dying of pneumonia at age twenty-nine.

220   ———. *A World I Never Made*. New York: Vanguard, 1936.
The first in a series of five novels about the O'Neill and O'Flaherty families, whose forebears were immigrant laborers in the nineteenth century. The story, opening in 1911 and set in Chicago, focuses on Danny, for whom the Irish church provides models of educated and ideological people—its nuns, priests, and teachers—in an environment of poverty and family tragedy. The sequels trace Danny's life as he becomes a writer: *No Star Is Lost* (1938), *Father and Son* (1940), *My Days of Anger* (1943), and *The Face of Time* (1953). All are published by Vanguard.

221   Gordon, Mary. *The Other Side*. New York: Viking Penguin, 1989.
Ellen Costelloe, angry at her father, steals money from his shop and comes to the "other side," America, specifically, New York. She works as a maid and a shopgirl for eight years, until she marries Vincent McNamara, another recent immigrant, who, as a skilled mechanic, is able to take her to live in the suburbs. But Ellen is never able to overcome the shame and anger of her youth and the circumstances of her immigration. After sixty-six years of marriage, she lies dying, surrounded by her surviving children and grandchildren. She and they privately recall their memories. Vincent comes home from the hospital in time to keep his promise that she could die in her own bed.

222   Kelly, Myra. *Little Aliens.* New York: Scribner's, 1910.
The third in the series of Miss Bailey stories.

223   ———. *Little Citizens: The Humours of School Life*. New York: McClure, Phillips, 1904.
The first in a series of humorous and touching stories about Constance Bailey, who immigrates to the U.S. as a child and becomes a teacher of Irish and Jewish immigrant children in a shifting neighborhood on the Lower East Side of New York. Miss Bailey attempts to help the children assimilate to American life without disparaging their cultural differences.

224 ———. *Wards of Liberty*. New York: McClure, Phillips, 1907.
The second in the series of Miss Bailey stories.

225 Kennedy, William. *Quinn's Book*. New York: Viking Press, 1988.
A historical novel about Danny Quinn, a fourteen-year-old famine immigrant, who lives in the Irish section of Albany, New York, and, wanting to be a journalist, records such events of his time (the 1850s and 1860s) as labor riots between Irish immigrants and native-born Americans for foundry jobs, and the New York City riots against conscription in the army during the Civil War, in which the Irish protest the exemptions that could be bought for $300, and the war in general, since the freed Negro slaves would become competitors for their jobs.

226 Marchand, Margaret. *Pilgrims in the Earth*. New York: Farrar and Rinehart, 1938.
Irish immigrants in "Vulcan," a Pennsylvania steel mill town, work among Jews, Poles, Italians, Chinese, Welsh and English, all maintaining their ethnic divisions and engaging in religious and nationality conflicts. All are oppressed by the German mill owner, Hugo Sturm, and when he is detained during World War I, his son inherits the business and makes some reforms.

227 McSorley, Edward. *Our Own Kind*. New York: Harper and Brothers, 1946.
In Providence, Rhode Island in 1916, Ned McDermott, an illiterate immigrant foundry worker, raises his orphaned grandson Willie to be educated, and teaches him Irish culture and legends. When Ned dies, the boy must quit school and go to work.

228 O'Connor, Edwin. *All in the Family*. Boston: Little, Brown, 1966.
A forceful and ambitious immigrant's son drives his three sons to be successful. James becomes a suave media priest and Charles an unscrupulous politician. Only Philip retains his integrity. The story is narrated by Cousin Jack.

229 Quigley, Father Hugh. *The Cross and the Shamrock; or, How to Defend the Faith*. Boston: Patrick Donahoe, 1853. Reprint, Upper Saddle River, NJ: Gregg, 1970.
Stories of the missionary priest Father O'Shane at his station in a New York farming community that borders Vermont. He

ministers to the famine immigrants working as day laborers on farms or on railroad gangs and getting low pay and no housing or food. The focus is on the O'Cleary family, who were driven from their County Clare home. The father having died from cholera aboard ship, the mother and children must fend for themselves as day workers on a farm, where they resist the pressure to convert to Protestantism. Two of the children die, but one becomes a priest and another a nun.

230 Sadlier, Mary Anne Madden. *Confessions of an Apostate; or, Leaves from a Troubled Life.* New York: Sadlier, 1864. Reprint, New York: Arno Press, 1977.

Simon Kerrigan immigrates to Boston in 1810 and gets a job in a hardware store. Advised to hide his Catholicism and pretend to be a Scot, he goes to night school, then moves to New Haven, where he marries his boss's daughter and has four children. His family in Ireland, learning of his deception, disown him, and when his only surviving son and wife discover his Irish background, they also reject him. He moves back to Boston, and, in 1844, heartsick after seeing his son leading a mob in attacking a Catholic church, he returns to Ireland.

231 Smith, Betty. *Maggie Now.* New York: Harper, 1943.

Patrick Dennis, a handsome pub dancer, escapes a compulsory marriage in County Kilkenny by sneaking off to Boston to take a job as a stable hand. He marries the unattractive daughter of his earlier Irish immigrant boss, who, having attained the middle class, is not pleased. They have one child, Maggie, who grows up unhappily and is deserted by her husband.

232 ———. *A Tree Grows in Brooklyn.* Philadelphia: Blakiston, 1943. New York: Harper and Brothers, 1947.

Francie Nolan, the daughter of an Irish immigrant and granddaughter of Austrian immigrants, grows up in poverty in an immigrant neighborhood in Williamsburg, Brooklyn. Though her father cannot support his wife and children as a pub singer who often drinks too much, she loves him, and, a good student, she manages to graduate from high school, go to college, and escape from poverty and tenement life.

233 Sullivan, James W. *Tenement Tales of New York.* New York: Henry Holt, 1895.

Stories about slum existence in New York in the 1890s. Those that deal with Irish immigrants are told in a "downtown Celtic" dialect. In "Slob Murphy" an incorrigible eight-year-old boy suffers a fatal injury, the result of a drunk's teasing him, and becomes almost angelic before his death. His funeral brings out the best in the neighbors. In "Minnie Kelsey's Wedding" a virtuous orphan living with a tyrannical uncle wins over a rich gambler. In "Cohen's Figure" Ernestine Beaulefoy, a model for fitting clothes, commits suicide after being humiliatingly handled by her boss. And in "Threw Himself Away" Legrant Brighton, a middle-class Irishman, marries a poor Jew and is disapproved of by his social club members; however, as his wife becomes the mainstay of their marriage because of his drinking and shiftlessness, her mother tells him that it is Rebecca who has thrown her life away.

234 Tully, Jim. *Shanty Irish.* New York: A. and C. Boni, 1928.

A realistic story about a poor immigrant Irish family through several generations. Hughie, a ditch digger, tells his grandson Jim stories of the famine years in Ireland, the hazardous crossing by ship to America, and the poverty of day laborers there. A constant frequenter of saloons, Hughie is a legendary raconteur of humorous tales about life in the Irish immigrant community. Jim describes his father's desertion of his children after their mother dies and their years spent in an orphanage until the oldest daughter, at thirteen, can provide for them.

235 Ward, Leo. *Holding Up the Hills.* New York: Sheed and Ward, 1941.

Connected stories set in the 1850s through the 1930s about Irish immigrants who escaped the potato blights and became farmers in Iowa. Their descendants lose the old sense of community as family life changes and the neighbors lose touch with their older culture.

Anthologies

236 Casey, Daniel J. and Robert E. Rhodes, eds. *Modern Irish-*

American Fiction: A Reader. Syracuse, N.Y.: Syracuse University
Press, 1989.

A collection of twenty-one pieces of fiction by Irish-American
writers, including those who wrote about immigrants: e.g., Kate
McPhelim Cleary, Finley Peter Dunne, Betty Smith, Mary Doyle
Curran, Edwin O'Connor, and Mary Gordon. The introduction
explains that the selection is based on the desire to illustrate the
effect of the transplantation of the new immigrants and of how the
later writers worked in the tradition of the earlier ones.

237   Fanning, Charles, ed. *The Exiles of Erin: Nineteenth Century
      Irish-American Fiction.* Notre Dame, IN: University of Notre
      Dame Press, 1987.

      Samples of fiction from three literary generations. Three
      excerpts are from the satiric fiction of the pre-famine immigrants
      before the 1840s: parodies of lawyers, political campaigns, Irish
      stereotypes, and popular sentimental fiction. Eight excerpts are
      from the "practical" fiction of the famine immigrants of 1850-
      1875: serious and didactic, concerning reasons for leaving
      Ireland, the difficulty of the passage by sea, and the problems of
      assimilating while keeping the Irish faith. And eight excerpts are
      from the children of those immigrants who wrote about the rise of
      Irish middle class between 1875 and World War I: from the urban
      slums to suburbs or prairie farms.

Secondary Sources

238   Casey, Daniel J. and Robert E. Rhodes, eds. *Irish-American
      Fiction: Essays in Criticism.* New York: AMS, 1979.

      Eleven critical essays on such writers as James T. Farrell and
      Edwin O'Connor and such subjects as "Women's Perspectives"
      and "Historical and Fictional Stereotypes of the Irish." The
      introduction states that the selection "demonstrates the scope and
      variety of the Irish community's experience in the United States,"
      and the arrangement of the essays places the writers of fiction in a
      "historical and social matrix." Includes a bibliography of fifty-two
      writers—their published novels, short fiction, and uncollected
      stories—and secondary sources.

239   Fanning, Charles. *The Irish Voice in America.* Lexington:
      University of Kentucky Press, 1990.

A historical and critical survey of Irish-American fiction from the 1760s to the 1980s, with a number of plot summaries. The literature is seen as a "uniquely American literature, one largely concerned with minority alienation and assimilation into a primarily urban New World environment" and as "one of the oldest and largest bodies of ethnic writing produced by members and descendents of a single American immigrant group." Includes a bibliography of primary and secondary sources.

240 *Irish-American Literature. MELUS* 18:1 (Spring, 1993).
Pertinent articles are on political novels and on Mary Doyle Curran, William Kennedy, and James T. Farrell.

ITALIAN

Individual Authors

241 Angelo, Valenti. *Golden Gate*. New York: Viking Press, 1939.
For young adults. Nino comes as a boy to the U.S., registering impressions of the sea voyage and his first sight of New York. In California he faces hazing by American boys.

242 ———. *Hill of Little Miracles*. New York: Viking Press, 1942.
For young adults. Ricco Santo, an immigrant boy with a limp, grows up in San Francisco in a community of Italians and Irish. After some conflicts, the two groups learn to appreciate and get along with each other.

243 ———. *The Rooster Club*. New York: Viking Press, 1939.
For young adults. The sequel to *Golden Gate*. Nino is a teen-ager and a boy scout and is accepted by the established Irish and Anglo groups of boys.

244 Arleo, Joseph. *The Grand Street Collector*. New York: Walker, 1970.
Immigrant Natale Sbagliato reluctantly accepts the political assignment of assassinating the radical editor of an Italian newspaper in New York City, who condemns Mussolini and the Fascist Party. He must then flee to Italy. His six-year-old son Pietro is in ignorance of the reason for his father's absence until

he is twenty and a college student, at which time he goes to Italy
to find his father.

245 Barolini, Helen. *Umbertina*. New York: Seaview Books, 1979.
     A four-generation novel focusing on the title character, a
brave and strong, if illiterate, woman, who comes from Calabria
to New York City with her older husband and three children.
After three years of poverty despite hard work, they join an Italian
enclave upstate, where she turns the provision of sandwiches to
laborers into a lucrative import business. Her daughters are
traditional and passive, but her great-granddaughter and
namesake, Tina, is spiritually restless in her financially secure
life, and visits her heroic grandmother's native village to see if she
can attain some of her purpose and spirit.

246 Benasutti, Marion. *No Steady Job for Papa*. New York: Vanguard
     Press, 1966.
     For young adults. Rosemary is the narrator of this family story
set in Philadelphia during World War I. Papa at 13 had come to
the U.S. to live with his sister but returned to northern Italy to
marry. Back in America, he earned money to send for his wife
and child, Rosemary. Instead of being the artist and scholar he
had hoped to be, he takes seasonal work in construction. When
Rosemary grows up, she helps support the family by working in
the mills and through her writing. She goes to business college,
they move to the suburbs, and there she marries an Irish-
American.

247 Bryant, Dorothy Calvetti. *Miss Giordano*. Berkeley, CA: Ata
     Books, 1978.
     Anna's parents, immigrants from northern Italy, move from
Vermont to Illinois to Colorado and to Montana, where her father
works in mines. When he contracts a lung disease, they move to
the Mission District in San Francisco. Anna is expected to work to
support her parents, but she continues in school, with the
assistance of teachers and scholarships, and becomes a high-
school English teacher. She remains at the same school for forty
years, teaching the children of new immigrants—Hispanics and
Asians—and Black migrants from the South.

248 Caruso, Joseph. *The Priest*. New York: Macmillan, 1956.

A story about Sicilians in Boston's West End and the role of the church in their lives.

249 Cautela, Giuseppe. *Moon Harvest.* New York: Lincoln Mac Veagh, Dial Press, 1925.

Romualdo and Maria come to New York from Tuscany with a growing family. She doesn't want to assimilate, happy enough to speak only Italian and take care of her home and children; but he does, studying English and American literature on his own and taking a second-generation Italian mistress. When Maria dies on a visit to Italy, he gives up his lover and focuses on being a father to his children.

250 Corsel, Ralph. *Up There the Stars.* New York: The Citadel Press, 1968.

Enrico and Maria Andrini come to New York, hoping to earn enough money to own their own land. But the 1930s depression puts Enrico out of work, and the family must live on the wages from Maria's sewing and son Frankie's sales of peanuts and newspapers on the streets. Frankie turns to petty crime, dreaming of being a gangster. Nearly killed in a gang war, he has a change of heart and looks to the stars for inspiration for a better life.

251 D'Agostino, Guido. *Olives on the Apple Tree.* Garden City, N.Y.: Doubleday, 1940. Reprint, New York: Arno Press, 1975.

Emile Gardella, a doctor, and his family, move out of their Italian immigrant community to blend in with the middle class; but Marco, the newly arrived young immigrant, believes in being himself and becoming an American in time, without giving up his Italian heritage.

252 De Capite, Michael. *Maria.* New York: John Day, 1943.

A three-generation novel set in Cleveland, narrated by Paul, the oldest child of Maria and Dominic Barone, both immigrants from Sicily but brought together through an arranged marriage in Cleveland. Dominic cuts himself off from other Italians, and, through foolish investments, loses everything in the 1929 crash and abandons his family. Maria works in sweatshops and becomes a union member. Paul resents his grandparents' old world values and social behaviors, because of how they have hurt his mother.

253 ———. *No Bright Banner*. New York: John Day, 1944.

A sequel to *Maria*, Paul Barone comes of age in the 1930s, disappointed with life in his tough community, where he has seen his best friend work for a racketeer and become a criminal. After working to support himself through college, he leaves Cleveland, though guilty about abandoning his mother, for Greenwich Village to live his own life and to feel like an American. Though he is disillusioned with America's capitalism, he desires to fight against fascism in World War II. Only afterwards can he return home to recognize the strength and value of his Italian roots.

254 De Capite, Raymond. *The Coming of Fabrizze*. New York: David McKay, 1960.

Augustine Fabrizze works hard for the railroads in Cleveland, hoping to save enough money to return to his village near Naples in some style. He becomes a foreman, then a successful shop owner. Because he is such an optimist and inspires others, his fellow immigrants invest together in the rising stock market. When they all lose everything in the crash of 1929, Fabrizze sells all he owns, shares his money with them, and moves to Chicago. Through the letters he sends his old friends, he continues to be an inspiration and eventually a legend for them.

255 ———. *A Lost King*. New York: David McKay, 1962.

A boy grows up in Cleveland's "Little Italy," where most of the immigrants work as laborers.

256 De Rosa, Tina. *Paper Fish*. Chicago: Wine Press, 1980.

A stream-of-consciousness novel in six parts which skip back and forth, about three generations of the Bellacasa family, from grandmother Doria's girlhood in Italy to an Italian neighborhood in a Midwestern city. Carmolina listens to her grandmother's stories and learns of her parents' adaptation to life in America, her father as a policeman.

257 Di Donato, Pietro. *Christ in Concrete*. Indianapolis: Bobbs Merrill, 1939.

Geronimo, an immigrant from the Abruzzi, working in the building trade in New York, is crushed to death, because his boss has used cheap materials and shoddy construction plans for his greater profit. Twelve-year-old Paulie takes over his father's job to support his mother and seven siblings; but he attends night school and refuses to accept that the exploitation of immigrants, at work and socially, cannot be changed.

258 ———. *Three Circles of Light*. New York: Julian Messner, 1960.
Seen through the eyes of fourteen-year-old Paolino Di Alva is this story of family life in an immigrant community. Father Geremio won't give up his American mistress; his wife, despite that, holds the family together. "La Smorfia" is a local faith healer and midwife who cures when the doctor can't and has more authority than the parish priest.

259 Fante, John. *Dago Red*. New York: Viking, 1940.
A series of autobiographical stories with a psychological emphasis about a son's conflicts with his immigrant father and the difficulty of being Italian and Roman Catholic in Denver during the depression of the 1930s.

260 ———. *The Wine of Youth: Selected Stories*. n.p., 1940. Reprint, Santa Rosa, CA: Black Sparrow Press, 1985.
A reprinting of stories from *Dago Red* as well as unpublished stories about his parents' youth in Denver and more stories based on his own youth.

261 Fast, Howard. *The Immigrants*. Boston: Houghton Mifflin, 1977.
In 1888 Joe Levette, a fisherman from San Remo, and his pregnant wife, Anna, sail to New York and are admitted through Ellis Island. They are cheated by earlier Italian immigrants and tricked into working in railroad camps in the West. Son Daniel is born in a boxcar. The family eventually arrive in San Francisco, where Joe buys a small fishing boat. After his death, young Daniel, through hard work and financial shrewdness, becomes rich, owning his own shipping company and marrying into a snobbish American family. The novel has several sequels.

262 Forgione, Louis. *The River Between*. New York: Dutton, 1928. Reprint, New York: Arno Press, 1975.
In a Sicilian immigrant colony in New Jersey, just across the river from New York, Demetrio is going blind. His son Orestes takes over his construction business, but he lacks the traditional

morality of his father. So does Orestes' wife Rose, also a second-
generation Italian, who wishes to be gone from the Italian
community. She takes an American lover and moves away, but
feels no more sense of belonging in her new environment than she
had in the old.

263   Fumento, Rocco. *Tree of Dark Reflection.* New York: Knopf,
       1962.
       Daniele Faustino grows up in poverty in Massachusetts with a
       brutal father whom he hates and fears. Drafted into the army and
       sent to Italy, Daniele visits his father's birthplace and learns that
       his father had intended to be a priest but lost his faith and married
       instead. Daniele comes to a clearer understanding and some
       acceptance of his father's behavior to his family.

264   Giardina, Denise. *Storming Heaven.* New York: Norton, 1989.
       Italian immigrants are minor characters in this novel about
       West Virginia and Kentucky coal miners and their attempts to
       form a union to protest the many injustices—including land theft,
       economic exploitation, and even murder—perpetrated against
       them by the owners.

265   La Polla, Garibaldi Marco. *The Grand Gennaro.* New York:
       Vanguard Press, 1935.
       Gennaro Accuci comes to the U.S. in the 1890s and starts a
       rag-and-scrap-metal business. By bullying others, including his
       friends, he becomes the owner of a large industry. His son dies as
       a soldier in the Spanish-American War. As a result, in a change of
       heart, Gennaro belatedly tries to help his friends, but they reject
       him and he dies a violent death.

266   La Puma, Salvatore. *The Boys of Bensonhurst.* New York:
       Norton, 1987.
       Seven stories set in a Sicilian community in New York
       between 1939 and 1943, the focus is on teenaged boys and young
       men.

267   Madalena, Lawrence. *Confetti for Gino.* Garden City: NY:
       Doubleday, 1959.
       Gino De Marino, one of a group of tuna fishermen in San
       Diego, tries to break away from the Sicilian immigrant colony,

which rigidly retains its old-world customs. He wants to be an American and marry an American woman.

268 Mangione, Jerre. *Mount Allegro*. Boston: Houghton Mifflin, 1943. Reprint, New York: Columbia University Press, 1981.

Lively and humorous stories about Gerlando Amoroso's growing up in a Sicilian immigrant community in Rochester, New York. The narrator stresses close knit family life and the camaraderie of the neighborhood. But when he is grown, the young man desires to live his own life as an American. To do so, he attends Columbia instead of his local university. After graduating, he goes to visit his family in Sicily and comes to a new appreciation of his heritage.

269 Marotta, Kenny. *A Piece of Earth*. New York: William Morrow, 1985.

One of the best of the Italian immigrant novels. In New York in the 1930s, Mike Buonfiglio ("good boy") and Agnes Zammataro, children of immigrants from different provinces of Italy, wish to marry. Her father refuses to allow her to choose her own husband, and Agnes refuses to accept Mike's obligation to take in his aging grandmother. Mike's genial Uncle Lino, a petty racketeer, his flighty mother Madge, and his stoically cheerful father Louie, and Agnes' simplistic mother and sardonically pessimistic father are other characters in the story. The grandmother, who had brought her eight young children to America after she was widowed and is still surprisingly hardy and willful, finally takes things into her own hands.

270 Pagano, Jo. *Golden Wedding*. New York: Random House, 1943. Reprint, New York: Arno Press, 1975.

A sequel to *The Paesanos*. At their golden anniversary party, with their children around them, the lives of Luigi and Marcella Simone are reviewed. They had been born in Italy but met in the United States. Frightened by the Mafia, they moved to Colorado, to Utah, and finally to California.

271 ———. *The Paesanos*. Boston: Little, Brown, 1940.

Episodes in the lives of the Simones, Italian immigrants in a mining community in Colorado, written with some attempt at giving the flavor of Italian-American dialect.

272 Panetta, George. *We Ride a White Donkey*. New York: Harcourt, Brace, 1944.

Humorous stories of the Caparuta family, immigrants from Calabria, on the East Side of Manhattan, written in Italian-American dialect.

273 Parini, Jay. *The Patchboys*. New York: Henry Hill, 1986.

Fourteen-year-old Sammy di Cantini lives in the "Patch," a shoddily built area for immigrant Italian, Welsh and Polish miners in a town on the Susquehanna River in Pennsylvania. In the summer of 1925, his older brother Vincenzo becomes a union organizer, partly as a result of his father's death in a mine accident, and Sammy visits his other brother, a petty gangster in New York. It is a summer of violence, and Sammy realizes that he must become educated in order to escape the fates of his father and brothers.

274 Petracca, Joseph. *Come Back to Sorrento*. Boston: Little, Brown, 1952.

Patsy Esposito works on the Brooklyn docks, planning to return to Sorrento to buy an olive grove. Instead he marries, takes in his wife's immigrant grandfather, has five children, and becomes a naturalized American citizen.

275 Piazza, Ben. *The Exact and Very Strange Truth*. New York: Farrar, Straus and Giroux, 1964.

At thirty-eight, Sicilian immigrant and shoemaker Carlo Gallanti woos and marries eighteen-year-old Veronica Dillman, of Baptist stock. He brings his Italian speaking mother and sister to live in his wife's small Arkansas town, and the Gallantis produce a large family. The townspeople harass them, and the Ku Klux Klan threaten to burn his shop, but through hard work and upright and fearless behavior, the family finally win the town's acceptance and even respect.

276 Pola, Antonia [Antonietta Pomilla]. *Who Can Buy the Stars?* New York: Vantage, 1957.

Marietta comes at age seventeen to Indiana in a marriage arranged by her parents to Sasso, an immigrant coal miner. Determined to become rich both for the sake of her children and to impress an Italian cousin of a higher social status, with whom she is in love, she starts a bootlegging business in her grocery store during the prohibition era. When she is forty and well off financially, she returns to Italy to impress her cousin, but he rebuffs her advances. Back home, her grown son and daughter are embarrassed by their mother's illegal past. Both leave home, andshe faces a life made empty and meaningless by her relentless pursuit of financial success.

277 Puzo, Mario. *The Fortunate Pilgrim*. New York: Atheneum, 1964.

Immigrant from Sicily, twice-widowed Lucia Santa Angeluzzi raises her six children by requiring the older ones to help support the younger. Larry gets involved with the syndicate; Octavia, frustrated in her desire to go to college, marries a Jewish student; and Vinnie sickens and dies from his work as a baker's assistant. Younger Gino steals coal for fuel from the railroad yard and plays in the streets until he is old enough to join the army. Prosperous Larry moves the family out of the ethnic neighborhood into a new home in the suburbs.

278 ———. *The Godfather*. New York: Putnam's, 1969.

A best seller and source of several popular Hollywood films. Vito Corleone, as a boy, flees to New York from Sicily after his father is killed by the Mafia. He marries and begins to raise a family, but beginning with self-protection, his fearlessness leads him to be the head of a syndicate in organized crime, including affiliations with the entertainment worlds in Las Vegas and Los Angeles. When he is injured in a coup by a rival gang, his son Michael, a war veteran who has tried to remove himself from the Italian community, is college educated and about to marry into a Yankee family, takes over the family business.

279 Savarese, Julia. *The Weak and the Strong*. New York: Putnam's, 1952.

Fortunata Dante's immigrant father was an impoverished intellectual who could not support his family. Like him is her husband, Joseph, who is kindly but ineffective and has trouble finding even temporary, unskilled work in New York City in the 1930s. Fortunata sees both of them as weak, and herself, upon whom her children must depend, as strong. She wants her children to be like her.

280 Tomasi, Mari. *Like Lesser Gods*. Milwaukee: Bruce, 1949.
     Pietro Dalli, from the Piedmont, is a stonecutter in Vermont.
An artist, he is devoted to his sculpture of memorial stones, but
his wife, wishing for them to open a little store together, because
she is fearful that he will die from silicosis, which he has
contracted from the stone dust, secretly ruins his masterpiece: a
stone cross with grape leaves. Yet he will not leave his work, and
he dies without regrets.

281 Vergara, Joseph R. *Love and Pasta*. New York: Harper and Row,
     1968.
     Pop comes to America from Calabria, dreaming of becoming
a great singer back in Italy, but he must work as a shoemaker.
After his son graduates from college and is about to be drafted
into the army during World War II, Pop decides at last to become
an American citizen.

282 Villa, Silvo. *The Unbidden Guest*. 1923. New York: Books for
     Libraries, 1970.
     Carlotto, who has grown up in Turin and graduated with
honors from the university there, comes to New Jersey to help
operate a silk farm. He falls in love with the American Gladys,
who beats him in tennis and is more interested in physical
activities than in lovemaking. Carlotto wavers between living in
Italy and in the United States: he fights for Italy in World War I
against the Austrians, but returns to America after the war.

283 Waldo, Octavia. *A Cup of the Sun*. New York: Harcourt, Brace
     and World, 1961.
     Pompei and Laura Rossi are the children of a prostitute and a
defrocked priest who left Italy after World War I. Andrea and
Niobe Bartoli are the children of immigrants Giovanna and Aldo,
who restores church artifacts. The young people grow up in a
poor Italian community in Philadelphia in the 1930s. When World
War II begins, the elders in the community are divided in their
loyalty, because some still have family in Italy. But the young
men enthusiastically join the armed forces, and the young women
wait for them. After the war, most of them realize that they do not
want to live as their parents have done. They will go to college
and become professionals.

Anthologies

284 Barolini, Helen, ed. *The Dream Book: An Anthology of Writings by Italian American Women*. New York: Schocken Books, 1985.
Includes poetry and essays as well as fiction (e.g., by Tomasi, Pola, Benasutti, Savarese, Bryant, and De Rosa) and an extensive critical essay by the editor, who wishes to make known, as others have not, that many Italian-American women have contributed to American literature and also documented immigrant and second-generation life in the U.S.

285 Tamburri, Anthony Julian, Paolo A. Giordano, and Fred L. Gardaphe, eds. *From the Margin: Writing in Italian Americana*. West Lafayette, IN: Purdue University Press, 1991.
In their introduction, the editors point out that this is the first anthology of its kind, and they describe what it means to be an Italian/American writer, deliberately not using the hyphen and explaining why such writers have often preferred to be considered mainstream. Includes fiction on the immigrant experience (among other genres) by Daniella Gioseffi, Helen Barolini, Tony Ardizzone, Kenny Marotta, and others. Also includes a few critical articles and a bibliography of primary and secondary works.

Secondary Sources

286 Cammett, John, ed. *The Italian American Novel*. Staten Island: American Italian Historical Association: Proceedings of the Second Annual Conference, October 25, 1969.
Talks by three Italian-American scholars on the history and the future of the novel and a panel discussion including the novelists Jerre Mangione, Ralph Corsel, and Joseph Vergara.

287 Finco, Aldo. "The Italian Americans: Their Contribution to the Field of Literature." *Ethnic Literatures Since 1776: The Many Voices of America*. Eds. Wolodymyr T. Zyla and Wendall M. Aycock. Lubbock: Proceedings of the Comparative Literature Symposium, Texas Tech University, Jan. 1976. 1X (1978): 1, 255-273.
A brief historical survey of Italians in America, explaining that because most immigrants were poor and often illiterate, it has

been only since the 1930s that important fiction has been written, and those stories focus on the alien who "has the faith to overcome obstacles and fulfill his destiny." Later writers, such as Puzo, stress the "alien's distinctive heritage in the interaction of the two cultures," which results in his becoming a part of American society.

288 Green, Rose Basile. "Italian-American Literature." *Ethnic Perspectives in American Literature: Selected Essays on the European Contribution.* Eds. Robert J. Di Pietro and Edward Ifkovic. New York: MLA, 1983.

Argues that, whereas there is a "distinctive quality" in Italian-American literature, it "evolved in tandem" with the literature of general American culture. The largest part of the essay is on prose fiction, and although there are references to a number of writers on immigrant themes, the emphasis is on contemporary and prominently popular writers like DeLillo and Gallico; however, Puzo is one of them.

289 ———. *The Italian American Novel: A Document of the Interaction of Two Cultures.* Teaneck, N.J.: Fairleigh Dickinson University Press, 1974.

A fairly comprehensive historical and critical survey, beginning with nineteenth-century immigrant autobiography, moving to the emergence of the novel, and ending with contemporary writers. Includes a number of plot summaries. That few women writers are paid attention to may have prompted Barolini's anthology and critical introduction on women writers.

290 *Italian-American Literature. MELUS* 14: 3-4, Fall/Winter, 1987.

Relevant articles are the following: Mary Jo Bona, "Broken Images, Broken Lives: Carmelina's Journey in Tina De Rosa's *Paper Fish*," which is about Italian-American women novelists and their development of a tradition that Tina De Rosa fits into; Fred L. Gardaphe, "Italian American Fiction: A Third Generation Renaissance," a brief history of Italian-American fiction, which leads to an illustration that the third-generation Italian-American writers, such as Jay Parini, Tina De Rosa, and Kenny Marotta, are returning to immigrant themes and situations in their fiction; Laurence J. Oliver, "The Revisioning of New York's Little Italies: From Howells to Puzo"; Flaminio di Biagi, "Italian-American

Authors: Notes for a Wider Categorization"; Richard A. Meckel, "The Not So Fundamental Sociology of Garibaldi Marto Lapolla"; and an interview with Pietro Di Donato, by Dorothée von Huene-Greenberg.

291 Peragallo, Olga. *Italian American Authors and their Contribution to American Literature*. New York: S. F. Vanni, 1949.

An early annotated bibliography of works by fifty-nine writers, with a short biography of each author.

JAPANESE (see also Asian)

Individual Authors

292 Buck, Pearl. *The Hidden Flower*. New York: John Day, 1952.

A Japanese woman marries an American soldier just after World War II and goes with him to live in Virginia; but the discrimination she faces there from his family and in their environs cause her to return to Japan, leaving her young son with an American friend, a woman doctor.

293 Charyn, Jerome. *American Scrapbook*. New York: Viking Press, 1969.

The Tanaka family is sent to Manzanar and Tule Lake internment camps. Each of the six members of the family tells the story from a different perspective.

294 Harada, Margaret N. *The Sun Shines on the Immigrant*. New York: Vantage, 1960.

A story of a hardworking immigrant family who achieve status and respect in Hawaii. Yoshio Mori flees his abusive father in Japan, works as a contract laborer in Hawaii for three years, and then as a chauffeur for a wealthy Anglo family in Honolulu. He and his picture bride Haru have two children. Yoshio has his own successful taxi business; son Jack, an engineer in sugar technology, is elected to the legislature; the daughter becomes a teacher. Throughout, the family praise Hawaii as their land of opportunity where Japanese, Koreans, Chinese, Portuguese, and native Hawaiians, as well as Caucasians live together in equality and harmony. All are enthusiastically patriotic Americans when the novel ends in 1938 with Yoshio and Haru planning their first trip back to Japan to visit their families.

295   Kadohata, Cynthia. *The Floating World.* New York: Ballantine, 1989.

In a story that switches back and forth in time, the narrator, Olivia, tells the history of her parents and immigrant grandmother, who had lived in Los Angeles before World War II, but became unsettled after the experience of the internment camps. They, she, and her younger brothers travel by car from place to place during the 1950s, looking for jobs and a home. They settle temporarily in Arkansas, where they get work as "sexers" in a chicken hatchery and then in Arizona, servicing and repairing candy machines. At eighteen, Olivia goes to Los Angeles to establish residency so that she can attend the state university, but her earlier experiences have made her permanently restless, and she sets out for some other place.

296   Kanazawa, Tooru. *Sushi and Sourdough: A Novel.* Seattle: University of Washington Press, 1989.

In 1895 Frank Yasuda immigrates to Seattle, but leaves to travel in California and Mexico. News of gold in Alaska brings him back, and he does well enough in the Yukon to return to Yokohama to bring back his children and wife, Yosu, and her parents and sister. They live for a while in eastern Washington state, where he owns a cigar and candy shop, but he decides to take his family to Juneau, where he buys a barber shop. The story ends in 1922 with his American-born son's departure for college.

297   Miyakawa, Edward. *Tule Lake.* Waldport, OR: House by the Sea, 1979.

In this novel based on the historical study by Dorothy Swaine Thomas and Richard S. Nishimoto, *The Spoilage* (1946), the narrator Ben Senzaki, a graduate of Harvard Law School and a lawyer in Sacramento, California, tells the story of his family and neighbors, mainly middle-class professionals living in the San Joaquin Valley just before World War II. His father, an immigrant at the age of eighteen in 1902, is a founder and member of the local Presbyterian church and a respected pharmacist, but because he is the publisher of a Japanese-American newspaper, is arrested after the bombing of Pearl Harbor. Eventually the whole family are sent to Tule Lake. Though brother Gordie enlists in the army, Ben and others become "no no boys," refusing to take loyalty oaths while they are being treated as criminals. When the war is over, Ben's parents go to Colorado, but Ben remains until all the inmates have been attended to.

298 Miyamoto, Kazuo. *Hawaii, End of the Rainbow.* Rutland, VT: Tuttle, 1964.

In the preface the author says that he was inspired by *Giants in the Earth* to do for Japanese immigrants what Rölvaag had done for Norwegians: write a fictional history of their experiences, focusing on a few families. Seikichi Arata, Adaki Mayeda, and Tarao Murayama, immigrants to Hawaii in the late nineteenth century, work on sugar plantations and marry picture brides. Their children become Americanized and American citizens after Hawaii becomes a U.S. territory, and one of them, Minoru Murayama, the narrator of the whole story, goes to San Francisco to become a medical doctor. He describes the geological, historical, social and political climates of Hawaii during his father's lifetime and of California in the 1930s and 1940s, as well as life in an internment camp, where he served as a camp doctor. After the war, he returns to Hawaii, where those of Japanese ancestry can feel more at home.

299 Mori, Toshio *The Chauvinist and Other Stories.* With an introduction by Hisaye Yamamoto. Los Angeles: UCLA, Asian American Studies Center, 1979.

Homey, authentic stories about the Japanese colony in Oakland, California during the 1930s and 1940s, some about the plight of aging immigrants among the assimilating second generation. Examples are "Miss Butterfly," in which two girls perform a Japanese dance for their father, but are anxious to get to their own American dance; "Operator, Operator," in which an old man in a boarding house can't get a gardening job any longer; and "The Travelers," in which young niseis leave their Utah internment camp, refusing to return to their pre-war homes and bound for all parts of the U.S. Mori was one of the first to write stories about Japanese-American life.

300 ———. *Woman from Hiroshima.* San Francisco: Isthmus, 1978.

An issei (first-generation) woman tells her grandchildren the story of her youth in Japan, her immigration to America and her life there until just after World War II.

301 ———. *Yokohama, California.* Caldwell, ID: Caxton Printers, 1949. Reprint, Seattle: University of Washington Press, 1985.
   Charming stories of issei and nisei in "Little Yokohama" in Oakland in the 1930s and 1940s: about nursery and flower shop workers, baseball games, and family and street life. With an introduction by William Saroyan to the first edition and by Lawson Inada to the second.

302 Murayama, Milton. *All I Asking for Is My Body.* San Francisco: Supa, 1959.
   Toshio Oyama and his younger brother Kiyoshi, the narrator, live next to an open ditch in the Japanese section for field workers in Hawaii. Their father has taught them that it is their duty to pay off the family debt. Toshio tries to rebel against this traditional family system, but eventually marries and settles into his father's pattern. Kiyoshi, however, after the attack on Pearl Harbor, joins the U.S. Army, wins enough money in a craps game to pay off the family debt, and is able to choose a life of individual freedom.

303 Okada, John. *No No Boy.* Rutland, VT: Tuttle, 1957. Reprint, Seattle: University of Washington Press, 1979.
   Nisei Ichiro returns to Seattle after two years in an internment camp and two years in prison for refusing to make a pledge of loyalty to the U.S. or be drafted into the army—being, that is, a "no no boy." Embittered, he feels loyalty neither to America—as his brother Taro does—nor to Japan—as his mother does. His friendships with Kenji, a nisei war hero whose legs were amputated, and Emi, deserted by her soldier husband, as well as the kindness of Mr. Carrick, who hires him despite his prison record, lead him to a reconciliation with his native country.

304 Sasaki, R. A. *The Loom and Other Stories.* St. Paul, MN: Graywolf, 1991.
   Interconnected stories about the lives of three generations of Japanese-Americans. Joanne Terasaki, the principal narrator, tells of her great-grandparents, the original immigrants and loyal U.S. citizens; her mother's inability to find professional work despite having graduated from college with honors; and her American-

born father's having been sent to Japan for his education (he is a "kibei"). The shadow of the internment camps hover over their post-war lives. Joanne and her two sisters grow up in an integrated neighborhood but are always concerned about "fitting in." One marries a Caucasian, and another decides to live in Japan.

305 Shirota, Jon H. *Lucky Come Hawaii.* New York: Bantam, 1965.

In this ironic and sometimes comic novel, Kama Gusada, a pig farmer, and his picture-bride Tsuyu live in Wailuku on the island of Maui, in a rural colony of other immigrant Okinawans. The Gusadas are loyal Japanese citizens, who have supported Japan with contributions of pigs for its war with China, and have sent a son to a university in Tokyo. The news of the Japanese bombing of Pearl Harbor arouses Kama's hopes that Japan will govern Hawaii and his son will get an important administrative post, and he paints the rising sun on his roof as a mark of loyalty. Meanwhile, his other children are attending Hawaiian schools, mingling with Chinese, Filipinos, Portuguese, and native Hawaiians, considering themselves Americans and refusing to learn Japanese. The youngest son wants to join the U.S. Army, and the mother worries that her sons will have to fight against each other.

306 ———. *Pineapple White.* Los Angeles: Ohara, 1972.

After immigrating to Hawaii from Hiroshima in 1906, working twenty years in the canefields and then as a gardener for a wealthy "haole" (white man), Jiro Saki, at sixty-five and a widower, decides to live in Los Angeles with his son Mitsuo, a World War II veteran who is married to the Caucasian Carole Sutterfield. Neither he nor Carole's mother has approved of the "mixed" marriage, and both want their ethnic traditions preserved in their grandchild, whom one calls Edward and the other Ichiro. Jiro takes a hotel room in Little Tokyo and meets Japanese-Americans who had been interned during the war and returned to a broken-down ethnic enclave to be prostitutes and gamblers or to manage shabby shops. He also befriends Negroes and poor whites. To his own surprise, after a life of strict rules, he feels at home among them, and he also finds that he and his family and Mrs. Sutterfield can achieve harmony together.

307 Sone, Monica Ito. *Nisei Daughter*. Boston: Little, Brown, 1953.
     An autobiographical narrative about growing up in Seattle in
     the 1920s and 1930s, with a great many details about the Japanese
     culture and attempting to accommodate it with being an American
     and struggling with discrimination. The story continues with vivid
     descriptions of the family's removal to an internment camp during
     the war and daily life there.

308 Sugimoto, E. I. *A Daughter of the Samurai*. Garden City, NY:
     Doubleday, Page, 1926. Reprint, Rutland, VT: Tuttle, 1966.
     An autobiographical novel about a young woman of a samurai
     family who comes to America and has to overcome the traditions
     of feudal Japan to fit into American life.

309 Uchida, Yoshiko. *Journey to Topaz*. New York: Scribner's, 1971.
     For young adults. Eleven-year-old Yuki is removed, with her
     family, to a relocation center in Topaz, Utah, at the start of World
     War II. Though she is frightened and saddened by the injustices
     suffered by herself and her family, she is also able to take
     pleasure in the new friends she makes and the fun they manage to
     have in the camp.

310 ———. *Picture Bride*. New York: Simon and Schuster, 1987.
     Hana Omiya sails to California to meet for the first time her
     husband, Taro Takeda, and is disappointed that he is much older
     than his photograph had suggested. In time, she falls in love with
     his younger friend, yet remains sexually loyal to her husband.
     Together they run a small grocery store in Oakland. Throughout
     their married life, they share in many tragedies: the deaths of
     friends—including the man she loves—and children from flu,
     accidents, and a shooting by American "patriots" during World
     War II. In the internment camp where they are sent during the
     war, Taro dies.

311 Wakatsuki, Jeanne Houston, and James D. Houston. *Farewell to
     Manzanar*. Boston: Houghton Mifflin, 1973.
     An autobiographical account of the internment experiences of
     Jeanne Wakatsuki and her family during World War II, including
     the stories of her immigrant parents in coming to America and her
     father's various attempts to support the family. Just as he becomes
     successful in the fishing industry, with his own boat, the war

begins, and he is arrested by the FBI. At Manzanar, the rest of the family keep busy with school and other activities, but the father is dispirited because his authority is weakened. He is never able to regain his former dignity. After the war, Jeanne continues to be haunted by a sense of shame for being Japanese, until visiting the abandoned camp and writing her memoirs relieve her of that burden and give her a new perspective on the unfair discrimination which was visited upon her people.

312 Yamamoto, Hisaye. *Seventeen Syllables and Other Stories.* Latham, NY: Kitchen Table Press, 1988.

Yamamoto is perhaps the first Japanese-American writer to gain attention from mainstream readers, her stories having appeared in some of the first multi-cultural anthologies. Most stories are set on the West Coast during the 1930s and 1940s and focus on the cultural gap between first- and second-generation girls and women: e.g. the title story and "Yoneko's Earthquake"; "The Legend of Miss Sassagawara," is set in an internment camp. Some are post-war and concern readjustment to a mixed society after life in the camps: e.g. "Epithalamium" (set in New York) and "Las Vegas Charley." The introduction is by King-Kok Cheung.

Anthologies

313 Mirikitani, Janice, ed. *Ayumi: The Japanese American Anthology.* San Francisco: Japanese American Anthology Committee, 1979.

Represented are four generations of Japanese-American writers of fiction. 1. isei: Ginko Okazaki; 2. nisei: Fred S. Kai, Taro Katayama, Toshio Mori, Ken Oshima, and Hisaye Yamamoto; 3. sansei: Robert H. Kono; and 4. yonsei, Geraldine Kudaka.

314 Okutsu, Jim, ed. *Fusion '83: A Japanese American Anthology.* San Francisco: San Francisco State University Press, 1984.

Fiction includes two stories from *Reimei*, a Japanese-American quarterly published in the 1930s and 1940s: the anonymous "Razzberries in Blue," in which the men refer to each other as "Japs" and search for light-skinned women to date; and Toshio Mori's "The Fruitpicker," in which an agricultural laborer takes pride in his son's being a U.S. soldier. The collection also includes Sheridan Tatsung's "Sake and Whispers," about a young Japanese woman who leaves her family to marry in the United States; Mr. Kokura, the arranger, tricks and forces her to be a prostitute in San Francisco. David Mas Masumoto's "Harvest Waters" concerns the neighboring grove farmers, one Armenian and one Japanese, who battle each other over water rights, though both are being cheated by an Anglo "ditchtender." Warren S. Kubata's "The Witch" is about an issei who teaches his grandson to be a Japanese chauvinist.

315 ———. *Fusion Two: A Japanese American Anthology.* San Francisco: San Francisco State University Press, 1985.

Eugene Tashima's "The Meeting" concerns a conflict between the first-generation farmers and a third-generation, real-estate agent who wants to turn their farms into office buildings. Yoshie Tao's "No More Dreams for Mr. Kashino" is about an issei migrant worker whose picture bride rejects him. Sumio Kubata's "The Apple" describes an issei widower living alone in the city. In Clyde Fugami's "The Fisherman's Wife" an old issei fisherman deals with the death of his wife by sailing out into the bay without supplies. Candace Osaka Ames and Louann Nosaka tell the story of an issei family in San Francisco who are fired from their jobs as gardeners and maids after the bombing of Pearl Harbor.

JEWISH

Individual Authors

316 Aleichem, Sholom [Sholom Rabinowitz]. *The Adventures of Mottel, the Cantor's Son.* New York: Abelard-Schuman, 1953. Translated from Yiddish by Tamara Kahana. New York: Collier Books, 1961.

An episodic and often humorous novel of thirty-nine chapters that describes the arranging for and travel from Russia of a few families to the U.S.: getting to Antwerp and London and celebrating Yom Kippur aboard the *Prince Albert*, with just potatoes, tea and bread. There is a detailed description of the chaos and fear in being processed through Ellis Island. Once in New York, they take American names, get jobs, and settle in. The narrator is the boy, Mottel.

317 ————. *Some Laughter, Some Tears: Tales from the Old World and the New.* Translated from Yiddish by Curt Leviant. New York: Putnam's, 1966.

Twenty tales, some about immigrants in New York.

318 Angoff, Charles. *Journey to the Dawn.* Cranbury, NJ: A. S. Barnes, 1951.

The first in a series of six novels, set between the turn of the century and 1935, about the fortunes of the Polansky family, who flee persecution in Czarist Russia and come to Boston in 1904. The sequel *In the Morning Light* focuses on second-generation David's education through high school and on his experiences as a soldier in World War I. *The Sun at Noon* deals with David as a student at Harvard and his estrangement from his parents and their old-world ways as well as on his experiences with discrimination. In *Between Day and Dark* David is a journalist in New York; in *The Bitter Spring* he works for a national magazine. *Summer Storm* (1963) concerns the Roosevelt New Deal Era and David's problems with ethnic intermarriage. All are published by Barnes.

319 Asch, Sholom *East River: A Novel.* Translated by A. H. Gross. New York: Putnam's, 1946.

In New York's East Side, among Jewish and Italian immigrant families, a saintly storekeeper raises two sons, one an invalid who becomes a scholar and the other an unscrupulous businessman.

320 ————. *The Mother.* New York: Horace Liveright, 1930. Reprint, New York: AMS Press, 1970.

A sentimental novel about an immigrant family from Poland, in which the mother is the center of their life. Her death throws them into chaos until the older daughter returns to care for the younger children.

321 ————. *Uncle Moses.* New York: Forwarts, 1918.

A prosperous manufacturer of clothing in a Polish village leaves with many of the villagers after a pogrom. In New York he opens another shop and employs many of his villagers. He wishes to marry the young daughter of one of them. She is forced to marry him although she hates him.

322 Astrachan, Sam. *An End to Dying*. New York: Farrar, Strauss and
     Cudahy, 1956.
         Jacob Kogan, a wealthy businessman in St. Petersburg,
     Russia, minimizes his Jewish background, speaking German,
     French, and Russian, but not Yiddish. When he is killed and his
     money is confiscated by the new Communist government in 1918,
     his family go to New York, where Uncle Lewis Cohen is an
     established businessman, and become successful garment
     manufacturers and merchant ship owners.

323 Bellow, Saul. *Mr. Sammler's Planet*. New York: Viking, 1970.
         Sammler, a journalist for a Polish newspaper in London,
     visits, with his wife, his home city of Cracow just before the
     outbreak of World War II. They are captured by the Nazis and
     shot at in a mass murder. Sammler escapes, joins the Jewish
     partisans and is almost killed by the Poles. His American nephew,
     Dr. Elya Gruner, helps Sammler and his daughter get to America
     after the war and helps provide for them there.

324 Berman, Henry. *Worshippers*. New York: Grafton, 1906.
         An Americanized, wealthy, middle-class married woman in
     Philadelphia wishes to become an actress and has a love affair
     with a newly arrived immigrant, who writes socialist poetry in
     Yiddish. She finds him not to be the romantic and adventurous
     man she had thought him, but priggish and stodgy instead; so she
     returns to her husband.

325 Bernstein, Herman. *Contrite Hearts*. New York: Wessels, 1905.
         Two sisters are followed to the U.S. by their atheist lovers,
     who live irresponsibly and abandon the women after a short time.
     Their rejected Orthodox suitors immigrate to the U.S. and marry
     the sisters. These relationships are more suitable, and the sisters
     are finally happy.

326 ———. *In the Gates of Israel: Stories of the Jews*. New York: J.
     F. Taylor, 1902.
         Tales of poor Jewish immigrants who struggle to maintain
     their cultural heritage.

327 Brinig, Myron. *Singerman*. New York: Farrar and Rinehart, 1929.
         The Singerman family from Russia immigrate to Minnesota,

where Father Moses becomes a peddler. In the 1920s, they move to "Silver Bow" (Butte), Montana, where the family run a small store. The children grow up and go separate ways.

328 ———. *This Man Is My Brother.* New York: Farrar and Rinehart, 1932.

A sequel to *Singerman,* which moves into the third generation, dealing with the problems that come with intermarriage, anti-semitism, and the loss of Jewish identity.

329 Brudno, Ezra S. *The Fugitive: Being Memoirs of a Wanderer in Search of a Home.* Garden City, NY: Doubleday, Page, 1904.

Israel, an orphan, is adopted by a Christian landowner. When he is grown, he leaves Kiev for the Lower East Side of New York, where he works in the sweat shops, rebels against orthodoxy, attends night school, and experiences the antagonism between uptown German Jews and the newer immigrants from Eastern Europe. Eventually he marries the daughter of his adoptive father.

330 ———. *The Tether.* Philadelphia: Lippincott, 1908.

A young man abandons his father to get an American education and marry an American woman, but both endeavors fail as does his attempt to reconcile with his father.

331 Bullard, Arthur [Albert Edwards]. *Comrade Yetta.* New York. Macmillan, 1913.

Based on a true story. Yetta Tayefsky immigrates from Russia to America as a little girl. She works in a garment sweatshop, eventually becoming a union organizer.

332 Cahan, Abraham. *The Imported Bridegroom and Other Stories of the New York Ghetto.* 1898. Reprint, New York: Garnet, 1968.

Ironic stories set in New York in the 1890s. In the title story rich Doctor Stroon returns to his village in Eastern Europe to get a Talmudic scholar to be the husband of his daughter Flora, who has become too Americanized. She rejects the young man at first, but comes to like him when he takes only a short time to become Americanized himself, preferring money and his radical intellectual associates to a study of the Talmud. As a result, her father is heartbroken. In "A Providential Match" Rouvke Arbel has become well-to-do after having been a contemptible servant in Russia, while his former master has become so impoverished that he sends his daughter to marry Rouvke. In "Circumstances" the law school graduate Boris Lurie cannot practice law in Russia, but it is no better in New York, where he can work only in a button factory. And in "A Ghetto Wedding" a young couple spend all their money on their wedding reception, hoping to garner many gifts, but nobody attends.

333   ———. *The Rise of David Levinsky.* 1917. Reprint, New York: Harper and Row, 1960.

When David's mother, who had wanted him to be a Talmudic scholar, dies in a Russian pogrom in 1882, he borrows money from the young woman he had planned to marry and goes to New York, where he quickly assimilates—shaving off his beard and giving up study of the Talmud. Though dreaming of getting a secular education at City College, he finds employment in a garment shop and fulfills another American dream as one who rises to become a wealthy manufacturer. But he cannot forget his past, and he remains lost between the two worlds.

334   ———. *Yekl, A Tale of the New York Ghetto.* 1896. Reprint, New York: Dover, 1970.

An ironic story in which a new immigrant outsmarts an older one. Shortly after Yekl Podkovnik leaves Russia and arrives in New York, he changes his name to Jake and otherwise becomes as American as possible. Working in a garment sweatshop and attending a dance hall at night, he meets and dates Mamie, also an Americanized immigrant. When Jake's wife Gitl and son arrive to join him, he is dismayed by her old worldliness and treats her badly, refusing to give up his mistress. Divorce ensues: Jake marries Mamie, and Gitl, with the settlement money, plans to marry and open a grocery store with Bernstein, a Talmudic scholar, who has been her boarder. The film *Hester Street* is based on this story.

335 Caspery, Vera. *Thicker Than Water.* New York: Liveright/Grosset and Dunlap, 1935.

In the 1880s the Pieras, Sephardic Jews whose ancestors were early immigrants, live in Chicago; daughter Rosa is about to marry a new German-Jewish immigrant. Another marries a new Polish-Jewish immigrant. The other Pieras look down on the new immigrants. In the 1920s, a granddaughter marries a new Russian-Jewish immigrant.

336 Cohen, Arthur A. *In the Days of Simon Stern*. New York: Random House, 1973.

A humble couple in Poland are told by a seer that their son Simon will become one of the thirty-six messiahs (of whom there is one for every generation). The family immigrate to the Lower East Side of New York. Simon grows up to be a financial wizard in real estate and becomes a millionaire. When he learns of that early prophecy, he establishes a community for Holocaust survivors. One of the inmates is a half-Jew, who was a collaborator in a concentration camp and who sets fire to the community.

337 Cohen, Hyman and Lester. *Aaron Traum*. New York: Liveright, 1930.

Eleven-year-old Aaron immigrates with his family in 1886 to New York, where, like the rest of them, he works in sweatshops. He becomes a union member and then a union organizer. His brother marries the factory owner's daughter. The two brothers clash over union-management negotiations. Their father is disappointed when their political concerns take all precedence over their cultural heritage.

338 Cournos, John. *The Mask*. London: Methuen, 1919.

Vanya Gombarov is born in Russia. With his family, he comes to Philadelphia, changes his name to John and wears a "mask" to deal with the pressures of having to be and look like an American. The sequel is *The Wall* (London: Methuen, 1921), which traces his life between twenty and thirty-one as a struggling journalist who has to support his family and therefore cannot marry his fiancé. Breaking off the engagement, he takes an assignment in London. In *Babel* (New York: Boni and Liveright, 1922), the third of the trilogy, John comes back to the U.S. and then returns to London at the start of World War I.

339 Ferber, Edna. *Fanny Herself*. New York: Stokes, 1917.

A partly autobiographical novel about a Jewish girl, Molly Brandeis, growing up in a Midwestern town, where her mother manages the family store. After her mother dies, Fanny goes to

Chicago to start her own business. While working for a mail order house, she wanders around the city sketching, marries a gentile childhood friend, and quits her job to take her art seriously.

340 Ferber, Nat J. *One Happy Jew.* New York: Farrar and Rinehart, 1934.

The Mamelstein family escape Hungarian anti-Semitism and comes to New York. Father Mayer becomes a millionaire; four of the sons change their names and marry gentiles. Only the fifth son, Pincus, retains his faith, marries a Jewish girl, becomes a schoolteacher in the East Side, and devotes his life to working among the poor Jews there. He is the only truly "happy Jew" of the family.

341 Fineman, Irving. *Hear Ye, Sons.* New York: Longmans, Green, 1933. Reprint, New York: Arno Press, 1975.

Joseph is conscripted out of his Polish village to serve in the Czar's army for five years. But brutalized by the other soldiers and realizing that his service could well be extended to twenty-five years, he escapes. With the help of an uncle in America, he manages to immigrate to New York, where, after a series of struggles with poverty and discrimination, he becomes a lawyer and raises children who become successful professionals. He makes sure that they know of the struggles which have enabled them to reach their present positions.

342 Frankel, A. H. *In Gold We Trust.* Philadelphia: William Piles's Sons, 1898.

Rich earlier immigrants exploit poor new ones in New York in the 1890s.

343 Fuchs, Daniel. *Summer in Williamsburg.* New York: Vanguard, 1936.

Philip Hayman is a twenty-year-old college student in an immigrant community in Brooklyn. His uncle is a gangster, his brother Danny the leader of a Jewish gang that fights Irish and Italian gangs; his father and mother are honest people who still honor their Jewish traditions. Philip struggles with the gap between the old and new customs and the strain of assimilation. The sequels are *Homage to Blenholt*, 1936, and *Low Company*, 1937; both focus on other members of the Jewish community. All were published by Vanguard and were republished in a single volume as *The Williamsburg Trilogy* in 1961, also by Vanguard.

344   Glass, Montague. *Abe and Mawruss: Further Adventures of Potash and Perlmutter*. Garden City, New York: Doubleday, Page, 1911.
    A sequel to *Potash*. More humorous tales about the two partners and the compromise of their cultural and ethical values in order to become rich.

345   ———. *Potash and Perlmutter*. Philadelphia: Henry Altemus, 1909.
    Humorous stories about two partners in the garment industry who take chances with the law to make money and barely escape getting in trouble. Told in Yiddish-English dialect.

346   Gold, Herbert. *Fathers: A Novel in the Form of a Memoir*. New York: Random House, 1967.
    Sam (Gold's father), at thirteen, runs away from his village in the Ukraine to avoid conscription in the Czar's army or a deliberate maiming to prevent that. In New York he works in a cigar factory for six years and is able to pay the transport to America for his brothers and sister; but his parents are killed in a pogrom before he can do so for them. He goes to Cleveland and, beginning as a peddler, becomes a successful store owner, then real estate investor, through the help of Schloimi Spitz, another immigrant, who rises to success in Las Vegas through managing a protection racket. The story is narrated by the son, who, divorced and an unemployed writer, feels that he has not lived as well as his father had.

347   Gold, Michael. *Jews Without Money*. New York: Liveright, 1930. Reprint, New York: Carroll and Graf, 1984.
    A Romanian immigrant and a Hungarian immigrant meet and marry in New York. Their son narrates this autobiographical novel about growing up in the poverty and depravity of the Lower East Side, with greedy landlords, gang members, pimps, prostitutes, perverts and drunks. The emphasis is on the advantage taken of the immigrant poor by the capitalist system and corrupt government, which are responsible not only for unemployment and evictions, but also for the corruption of rabbis, his father's

illness from paint fumes and his sister's being trampled to death
by a horse cart while she is collecting wood in the streets for fuel.
Gold states that he wrote the book to counter attack Hitler's false
claims about universal Jewish wealth and power.

348 Goldreich, Gloria. *Leah's Journey*. New York: Harcourt Brace
     Jovanovich, 1978.
     Leah and David Goldfeder marry after their respective
spouses have been murdered in a pogrom in Odessa and
immigrate in 1919 to New York. A promising clothing designer,
Leah becomes a forelady at a dress factory and gets involved in
union activity through her love affair with Eli Feinstein. Eli dies a
hero in a fire modeled after the Triangle Shirtwaist Company fire
of 1911. David works as a pants presser by day and attends night
school, finally winning a scholarship and becoming a psychiatrist.
Leah's brother Shimon Hartstein changes his name to Seymour
Hart and becomes a wealthy manufacturer of ready-to-wear
women's clothes, and Leah is his chief designer. Through her
travels to Paris fashion shows, she becomes part of an
organization to bring Jewish refugees from Hitler's Europe to the
United States.

349 Halper, Albert. *On the Shore: A Young Writer Remembering
     Chicago*. New York: Viking Press, 1934.
     In these autobiographical short stories, a writer looks back
nostalgically on his days as a boy among Lithuanian Jewish
immigrants in Chicago.

350 ———. *Sons of the Fathers*. New York: Harper and Brothers,
     1940.
     Saul Bergman hides in boxcars and bribes border guards to
escape military conscription in Lithuania in 1892. He comes to
Chicago and in time is able to own a small grocery store. When
World War I breaks out, Saul is a pacifist. He helps his older son,
Ben, to escape the draft by managing to get him war work as a
civilian. Younger son, Milt, however, joins the army and is killed
in France.

351 Helprin, Mark. *Ellis Island and Other Stories*. New York: Dell,
     1981.
     The title story, a satiric fantasy, concerns a Jewish scholar

who is detained at Ellis Island because he proclaims that he is an anarchist and is employed as a cook's helper. Once in New York he attends art school, then takes a series of jobs, including one in a tailor shop.

352 Hurst, Fannie. *Humoresque*. New York: Harper and Brothers, 1919.

A collection of short stories, some about second-generation German Jews who have become successful businesspeople and some about the aspirations of the third generation to become successful artists.

353 ———. *Just Around the Corner: Romance en Casserole*. New York: Harper and Brothers, 1914.

A collection of short stories, previously published in magazines, about New York working girls, treated with sympathy and humor.

354 Kussy, Nathan. *The Abyss*. New York: Macmillan, 1916.

An orphaned immigrant boy learns how to support himself through petty crime on the streets.

355 Lessing, Bruno [Rudolph Block]. *Children of Men*. New York: McClure, Phillips, 1903.

A collection of twenty-three stories about ghetto life in New York, told with wry humor and pathos about the interaction of hopeful new arrivals and disillusioned earlier immigrants. For instance, "A Rift in the Cloud" concerns a Hungarian Jew who is ostracized because of his family's seamy reputation in the old country; "End of the Task" is about a girl in a sweatshop remembering her girlhood in Russia; and "The Americanization of Shadrack Cohen" is about a father who uses reverse psychology on his sons by pretending to embrace American values so that they will rebel and revert to orthodox traditions.

356 ———. *With the Best Intention*. New York: Hearst's International Library, 1915.

More stories in the ghetto setting, with less pathos and more humor, mainly about Lapidowitz, who comes to Ellis Island with seventy-six dollars in cash and lives off other Jews, while he waits to marry a rich woman.

357 Levin, Meyer. *The Old Bunch*. New York: Viking Press, 1937.
     About twenty second-generation boys and girls growing up on
the West Side of Chicago, from 1921 to 1934, from adolescence
to their thirties, and the conflicts they have with their first-
generation parents, because they see their peers as more important
than their parents and American culture as more attractive than
the old-world culture which their parents wish to retain.

358 Levitin, Sonia. *Silver Days*. New York: Macmillan Atheneum,
     1989.
     For young adults. The Platt family have escaped from Nazi
Germany in the 1930s and come to New York. (The story of their
flight to Switzerland and then voyage to the U.S. is told in a
preceding novel, *Journey to America*, Macmillan, 1970.) Papa
and Mama, used to a middle-class life, must work at menial jobs
to support their three daughters, who want desperately to be
accepted as Americans. As the war in Europe approaches, they all
have a great deal of apprehension. Papa decides to take the family
to California, where there may be better opportunities.

359 Lewisohn, Ludwig. *The Island Within*. New York: Harper and
     Brothers, 1928. Reprint, Philadelphia: Jewish Publication Society
     of America, 1968.
     Arthur Levy, the son of wealthy German-Jewish immigrants,
grows up, graduates from Columbia, becomes a doctor, and
marries the daughter of a Protestant minister. Neither Arthur nor
his sister Hazel has been taught anything about their Jewish
heritage, but his parents have disapproved of their children's
marriages to gentiles. After Arthur experiences discrimination
from both his gentile friends and his wife and learns about his
heritage and embraces it, his marriage begins to fail. He does
volunteer work at a Jewish hospital, finally going to Romania at a
rabbi's request to investigate anti-Semitism there and to help
Romanian Jews with their medical problems.

360 Malamud, Bernard. *The Assistant*. New York: Farrar, Strauss and
     Cudahy, 1957.
     Martin Bober escapes the draft in his native Russia and
immigrates to New York, where he opens a little grocery store,
which never makes much money. He lives a dreary existence
above it with his wife Ida and daughter Helen. Italian-American

Frankie Alpine comes to be his assistant, and, after Martin's death, converts to Judaism and takes over the shop.

361 ———. *Idiots First.* New York: Farrar, Strauss, and Giroux, 1963.

Three in this collection of stories are about immigrants: the title story, "The Jewbird," and "The German Refugee."

362 ———. *The Magic Barrel.* New York: Farrar, Strauss and Cudahy, 1958.

Some of these stories are about immigrants: e.g., Feld, the shoemaker in "The First Seven Years"; retired egg candler Kessler in "The Mourners"; and Manischevitz in "Angel Levine." Immigrants also figure in "The Bill," "The Loon," "Take Pity," and "The Magic Barrel."

363 Nyburg, Sidney. *The Chosen People.* Philadelphia: Lippincott, 1917.

Rabbi Philip Groetz, of a rich and Americanized Baltimore synagogue, moved by religious principles, tries but fails to bring together the uptown middle-class German Jews and the recent, Eastern European and poor, downtown Jews. However, Russian-born labor leader David Gordon, is successful, using political principles, in leading the downtown Jews in a protest against their employers.

364 Olsen, Tillie. *Tell Me a Riddle.* New York: Delacorte, 1960.

As an old woman is dying, she recalls her youth in Europe, her immigration and marriage, and the raising of her children—always living according to the needs of others. Her granddaughter wants to hear her stories and supports her in her refusal to move, with her husband, to a retirement home. The story is told in stream-of-consciousness narration.

365 Oppenheim, James. *Dr. Rast.* New York: Sturgis and Walton, 1909.

A German-Jewish doctor works among the poor, Eastern European immigrants on the Lower East Side, where there is a shortage of doctors. A girl from the neighborhood attends college and medical school at great sacrifice for her family, but once she has her degree, she turns her back on her people, ashamed of their peasant ways and poor English. Dr. Rast shames and reforms her.

366 ———. *The Nine-Tenths*. New York: Harper and Brothers, 1911.
Joe Blaine, editor of a pro-labor journal, espouses the cause of working people, particularly Jews and women. He helps to organize the union, promotes a women's strike against the garment industry, and rescues some of the victims of a factory fire, which is based on the Triangle Shirtwaist Company fire of 1911.

367 Ornitz, Samuel. *Haunch, Paunch, and Jowl: An Anonymous Autobiography*. New York: Boni and Liveright, 1923.
Meyer Hirsch, son of immigrants, realizes as a boy that, if he is to succeed, he must choose the American, not the Jewish way. He quits Hebrew school and becomes a gang member, selling protection to shopkeepers. He attends college and law school, and, as a lawyer, works for Tammany Hall, eventually becoming a judge of the criminal court. His friend Lazarus Cohen changes his name to Lionel Crane and goes to Harvard to become a doctor.

368 Ozick, Cynthia. *The Cannibal Galaxy*. New York: Knopf, 1983.
Joseph Brill is a French Holocaust survivor, whom, as a boy, nuns had hidden in the basement of a convent in Paris, where they brought him books for his education. He immigrates after the war to the Midwest, where he becomes the principal of a school. He hopes to make a difference in the world through recognizing genius and promoting the truths he knows. But he is disappointed by the mediocrity of his students and he misses the one opportunity in his life to recognize a brilliant student, by allowing himself to be deceived by her mother.

369 ———. *The Pagan Rabbi and Other Stories*. New York: Knopf, 1969.
The title story, "Envy; or Yiddish in America," "The Suitcase," and "Virility" are about immigrants.

370 ———. *The Shawl: A Story and a Novella*. New York: Knopf, 1989.
The very short and concise title story is about the murder of Rosa's baby in a concentration camp and the shawl that once

wrapped her. The companion piece is "Rosa," a novella about the mother, who survived the Holocaust but thirty years later in Florida imagines that Magda, grown, has come back to her and talks to her.

371 Paley, Grace. *The Little Disturbances of Man.* New York: Viking Press, 1956.

In this collection of New York stories, "Goodbye and Good Luck," "The Loudest Voice," and a few others are about immigrants. About half of the other stories are about second- and third-generation Jews.

372 Potok, Chaim. *The Chosen.* New York: Simon and Schuster, 1967.

Two Yeshiva students—Danny Saunders and Reuven Malter—are caught up in struggle between two Hasidic sects: the ultra-orthodox and the more liberal Misnagdim.

373 ———. *In the Beginning.* New York: Knopf, 1975.

Max Lurie served as a Polish soldier, being continually persecuted by the Christians. After the war, he endured a pogrom in which his uncle was murdered. As an immigrant in New York, he sees his son David persecuted by Polish-American boys who hate Jews. David fantasizes about being a hero of his people. As a teenager when World War II ends, David learns, with great sorrow, about the deaths of family members in the Holocaust.

374 ———. *My Name Is Asher Lev.* Greenwich, CT: Fawcett, World, 1972.

In the Crown Heights section of Brooklyn, Asher's grandfather is a celebrated Hasidic leader from Russia; both his mother and father work on behalf of Jewish causes and Hasidic learning. But Asher wants to be an artist in the Western tradition. His family and indeed the whole community disapprove and demand that he either give up the vocation or leave the community.

375 Reznikoff, Charles. *Family Chronicle.* New York: Universe Books, 1971.

Young Russian-Jewish Sarah Yetta Volsky comes at the turn of the century to New York, hoping to get an education, but must work in a sweatshop. She marries and lives a life of poverty. Her hopes for higher education for her son Ezekial are also frustrated: he goes to high school and then runs a small bookshop in Greenwich Village.

376 Rogin, Gilbert. *What Happens Next?* New York: Random House, 1971.

A young man wants to write the biography of his father, an immigrant from Latvia.

377 Rosenfeld, Paul. *The Boy in the Sun.* New York: McCauley, 1928.

David is brought up, in the 1920s, in a wealthy German-Jewish family among mostly gentiles in Harlem. His father tells him that their family are more like gentiles than like the new immigrants, Eastern European Jews, whom he considers shameful. The boy is sent to a private school, but there he is taunted by the other boys and the principal for being Jewish, and he realizes that he cannot and should not consider himself as apart from other Jews.

378 Rosten, Leo [Leonard Q. Ross]. *The Education of H*y*m*a*n K*a*p*l*a*n.* New York: Harcourt, Brace, 1937.

Humorous stories about Mr. Parkhill and his adult immigrant students learning English in night school in New York in the 1930s. His most challenging student is the irrepressible Hyman Kaplan from Kiev, who tries very hard to be an American and to impress his teacher. Despite his very obvious shortcomings as a student, Kaplan is always optimistic and confident in his abilities.

379 ———. *The Return of H*y*m*a*n K*a*p*l*a*n.* New York: Harper and Brothers, 1959.

More stories about the night school adventures of Mr. Parkhill and Mr. Kaplan.

380 Roth, Henry. *Call It Sleep.* New York: Ballou, 1934. Reprint, New York: Avon, 1964.

Young David Schearl and his mother Genya are met at Ellis Island by his father Albert, who has been working as a printer in New York's Lower East Side. Thinking that the boy is not his son, Albert tyrannizes them. David also has a hard time adjusting to the tough life of the streets, as well as to the poorly run Hebrew school, which he must attend. After an accident in which David almost dies, his father accepts his paternity. Written with some Yiddish-English dialect.

381 ———. *Mercy of a Rude Stream.* New York: St. Martin's Press, 1994.

The first volume in a series of six (the other five written but yet to be published) is subtitled "A Star Shines Over Mt. Morris Park." Shifting between the voices of the boy Ira Stigman and the old Ira writing his memoirs, the narration traces the life of Ira from age eight to fourteen, from 1916 to 1922. He lives in an extended immigrant family on the Lower East Side and then in Harlem, where he is persecuted by gentile boys.

382 Sachs, Emanie [Mrs. Augustus Philips]. *Red Damask.* New York: Harper and Brothers, 1927.

In the early part of the century, Abbey Hahl's upper-middle-class German-Jewish parents impose upon her a strict code in order to emphasize their genteel social status. They refuse to let her go to college or to move with her husband to Texas. Meanwhile, despite their pretensions, the family are excluded from gentile clubs and social affairs.

383 Sachs, Marilyn. *Call Me Ruth.* New York: Doubleday, 1982.

For young adults. Eight-year-old Rifta and her mother Faigel Zelitsky, living in Czarist Russia, get ship tickets to the U.S. from their father Shmuel, who has been working in a New York tailor shop for eight years. In New York, Rifta becomes Ruth and Faigel, Fanny, as their relatives persuade them not to look or act like greenhorns. Shmuel (Sam) dies soon after they arrive, and Fanny must work in a sweatshop, though she misses her parents and wants to go back to Russia. But Ruth loves America and her American teacher, whom she wants to please and emulate. Ashamed of her mother, Ruth is especially angry and embarrassed when Fanny gets mixed up in the new union, goes on strike and is arrested. But others recognize Fanny as a hero. Fanny becomes an effective union organizer.

384 Schneider, Isidor. *From the Kingdom of Necessity.* New York: Putnam's, 1935.

Morris Hyman and his family, including five-year-old Isaac,

leave their Polish village in 1900 for New York, where Morris gets then loses his factory job and becomes a janitor, while his wife takes in boarders. Isaac rejects his father's religious orthodoxy, and though he wants to be a writer, because of his pacifism during World War I, which leads to his involvement in the labor unions, he does not go to college but decides to remain in the working class.

385   Seide, Michael. *The Common Thread.* New York: Harcourt, Brace, 1944. Reprint, New York: Arno Press, 1975.
      Stories set in an immigrant community in East Flatbush, Brooklyn.

386   Singer, Isaac Bashevis. *A Crown of Feathers.* New York: Farrar, Strauss and Giroux, 1974.
      About half of these stories are set in Polish villages and the other half in New York and are about Jewish refugees from the Nazis. All deal with the supernatural—e.g., dybbuks and ghosts—in contemporary life.

387   ———. *Enemies: A Love Story.* New York: Farrar, Strauss and Giroux, 1972.
      Herman Broder, a Holocaust survivor in New York, is employed by a rabbi as a ghostwriter, but he poses as a book salesman. He also has two women, neither of whom knows about the other: one is Yadwiga, a Polish peasant who saved his life during the war; the second is his mistress, Masha. Unexpectedly, his wife Tamara, whom he thought had died in Europe, shows up.

388   ———. *Passions and Other Stories.* New York: Farrar, Strauss and Giroux,1975.
      Stories similar to those in *A Crown of Feathers.*

389   Steiner, Edward. *The Broken Wall.* New York: Fleming H. Revell, 1911.
      A collection of stories about immigrant life in the tenements of the Lower East Side.

390   ———. *The Mediator.* New York: Fleming H. Revell, 1907.
      After his mother dies, Samuel Cohen is raised by a Catholic Russian nurse. When a young man, he enters a monastery to

become a priest. But after he witnesses a Christian pogrom against the Jews, he flees to the U.S., where he becomes a Christian evangelist to the Jews of the Lower East Side and marries the daughter of a missionary colleague.

391 Sterner, Lawrence. *The Un-Christian Jew.* New York: Neale, 1917.

Rabbi Cordova, disgusted by the uptown German-Jews' treatment of the downtown Eastern-European Jews, establishes a utopian community based on what he believes to be the true teachings of Christ.

392 Tobenkin, Elias. *The House of Conrad.* New York: Stokes, 1918. Reprint, Ridgewood, NJ: Gregg, 1971.

A three-generation novel about the assimilation of an immigrant family. The son becomes a labor leader; the grandson rejects his father's values and becomes an independent worker.

393 ———. *Witte Arrives.* New York: Stokes, 1916. Reprint, Ridgewood, NJ: Gregg, 1968.

Emil Wittowski, as a child of seven, comes in the 1880s from Russia to New York, where his father supports the family as a peddler. Emil works hard to be educated and become a writer. He changes his name to Witte, graduates from a Midwestern university, and becomes a journalist, but his gentile colleagues do not accept him socially. He marries an American Protestant woman, but their cultures clash and they grow apart. Uncle Simon escapes from Siberia and converts Emil to socialism, and Emil becomes the editor of a liberal weekly.

394 Wallant, Edward Lewis. *The Pawnbroker.* New York: Harcourt, Brace and World, 1961.

Sol Nazerman, an art historian, has survived the Nazi concentration camp in which his wife and children were killed. In Harlem he runs a pawnshop apathetically and helps support his sister and her family, who attempt social mobility by disguising the fact that they are Jews. Sol's apathy is broken when his assistant, a young black man, dies saving his life. A motion picture of the same name is based on this novel.

395 Weidman, Jerome. *Fourth Street East: A Novel of How It Was.*
New York: Random House, 1970.
Joseph Kramer, the narrator's father, leaves his Eastern
European village and comes to New York in 1914. He spends
much of his time and money helping European Jews in need to
come to New York. Rather than being considered the saint his son
believes him to be for his selflessness, others consider him a
simpleton. The son tells other stories about immigrants and what
it was like to grow up in their community.

396 Yezierska, Anzia. *Bread Givers.* Garden City, NY: Doubleday,
Page, 1925. Reprint, New York: Persea Books, 1975.
Subtitled "A struggle between a father of the Old World and a
daughter of the New," this novel focuses on the lives of
immigrant Jewish women at the beginning of the century. Sara
Smolensky breaks away from her domineering father, who has
made his daughters support him, while he stays home to study the
Talmud, and has arranged their marriages according to how well
the husbands can provide for him. She leaves home, supporting
herself while she goes to night school. Winning a scholarship, she
is able to graduate from college and become a teacher. She
marries a man she loves and then, seeing her father alone and
poor, is finally able to forgive him. The introduction is by Alice
Kessler Harris.

397 ———. *Children of Loneliness.* New York: Funk and Wagnells,
1923.
Stories focusing on the difficulties experienced by immigrant
women. The title story concerns a second-generation young
woman who can feel at home neither in the world of her
immigrant parents nor among the Americans of her new society.

398 ———. *Hungry Hearts.* Boston: Houghton Mifflin, 1923.
Reprint, Salem, NH: Ayer, 1984.
Another collection of stories focusing on immigrant women,
some of whom, like Shenah Pessah in the title story, yearn for the
good things of American life, like education and romance. "The
Fat of the Land" concerns Hannah Breinah, whose successful
grown-up children move her to a fancy high-rise apartment,
where she feels ill at ease, missing her Lower East Side shops and
neighbors.

399 ———. *Salome of the Tenements*. New York: Boni and Liveright, 1923.

Based on the marriage of the author's friend and a socialist writer to the son and heir of an upper-class WASP family, this story has as its heroine Sonya Vronsky, a reporter for her community newspaper. She falls in love with the wealthy John Manning, who, because of her, will devote his life to social causes.

Anthologies

400 Angoff, Charles and Meyer Levin, eds. *The Rise of Jewish American Literature. An Anthology of Selections from the Major Novels*. New York: Simon and Schuster, 1970.

In the introduction, the editors point out that Jewish fiction has become popular among mainstream readers. Selections from Cahan, Angoff, Henry Roth, Lewisohn, Fuchs, Meyer Levin, Malamud, and Herbert Gold.

401 Chapman, Abe, ed. *Jewish-American Literature: An Anthology*. New York: New American Library, 1974.

In the introduction Chapman states that Jewish-American writers were, until the fifties and sixties, seen as aliens in the "prevailing American culture unless the writing had nothing to do with Jews or anything Jewish."

402 Eisenberg, Azriel, ed. *The Golden Land: A Literary Portrait of American Jewry, 1654 to the Present*. New York: Thomas Yoseloff, 1964.

A collection of mostly very short pieces of autobiography, fiction, essay and poetry, arranged into ten divisions. Relevant fiction appears in seven of these: I. "Beginnings," with Israel Zangwill's "Noah's Ark"; II. "Pioneering Days," with John Uri Lloyd's "A Journey with Old Mose," and Cahan's "A Greenhorn's First Day in America," from *David Levinsky*; III. "Ghetto," with Henry Roth's "East Side Cheder," from *Call It Sleep*, Samuel Ornitz's "Catching Souls," from *Bride of the Sabbath*, Charles Reznikoff's "In Business for Himself," from *By the Waters of Manhattan*, a selection from Yuri Suhl's *One Foot in America*, Z. Lubin's "Mr. Harkin's Lots," and Jerome Weidman's "Old Clothes for Poland"; V. "Second Generation," selections from Charles

Angoff, Herman Wouk, and Anzia Yezierska; VI. "Hostility," with selections from Sam Ross, Yezierska, and Arthur Miller; and VII. "War," with selections from Albert Halper, Louis Falstein, and Irwin Shaw. The divisions are preceded by a discussion of the social and historical settings for each period.

403 Gross, Theodore, ed. *The Literature of American Jews.* New York: Free Press, 1973.

Selections of fiction and poetry in three sections: 1. "Early Literature and the East European Migration"; 2. "Between the Wars"; and 3. "After the War—A Creative Awakening." The introduction explains the social and historical settings.

404 Howe, Irving, ed. *Jewish America Stories.* New York: New American Library, 1977.

A collection of twenty-six stories, with a historical and critical introduction by the editor: "not all of the stories in this collection deal with the immigrant Jewish milieu, but almost all of them bear its stamp. . . ."

405 Malin, Irving and Irwin Stark, eds. *Breakthrough: A Treasury of Contemporary American-Jewish Literature.* New York: McGraw, Hill, 1964.

With a critical introduction by the editors, who propose that a group of Jewish-American authors have become part of the mainstream of American literature.

406 Walden, Daniel, ed. *On Being Jewish: American Jewish Writers from Cahan to Bellow.* Greenwich, CT: Fawcett, 1974.

A critical essay by the editor precedes this collection of writings on Jews in America and their experiences. All reflect the Jewish immigrants' hopes and problems, which have influenced their descendants.

Secondary Sources

407 Chametzky, Jules. *Our Decentralized Literature: Cultural Meditations in Selected Jewish and Southern Writers.* Amherst: University of Massachusetts Press, 1986.

Comments on Cahan, Michael Gold, Henry Roth, Singer, and others.

408 Fine, David M. "Attitudes Toward Acculturation in the English Fiction of the Jewish Immigrant, 1900-1917." *American Mosaic: Multi-cultural Readings in Context.* Eds. Barbara Roche Rico and Sandra Mano. Boston: Houghton Mifflin, 1991, 76-87.

Fine believes that Tobenkin's *Witte Arrives*, Brudno's *Fugitive*, and Steiner's *Mediator* affirm total assimilation; and Nyburg's *Chosen People* illustrates the frustration of attempted assimilation. But Cahan's *David Levinsky* is the only early immigrant novel to show the pain and loss that come with assimilation or success for the immigrant: it portrays "realistically the ironies, complexities, and dilemmas of cultural assimilation." It is, partly on that basis, superior to the others.

409 ———. *The City, the Immigrant, and American Fiction, 1880-1920.* Metuchen, NJ: Scarecrow Press, 1977.

Begins with a discussion of the nativist and pro-immigrant views of the changing ethnic make-up of American cities and proceeds to a listing, with plot summaries and analyses, of tenement tales, representations of the ghettos, and the immigrant labor novel. The emphasis is heavily upon Jewish writers, and Abraham Cahan is treated in detail in a special chapter. The afterword suggests that the immigrant novel is the "father of the modern ethnic novel." Includes a bibliography of novels, short stories, and secondary books, articles, and reviews.

410 Fried, Lewis. *Handbook of American-Jewish Literature: An Analytical Guide to Topics, Themes, and Sources.* New York: Greenwood, 1988.

Of particular note are Sections 1, 2, and 3, which treat American-Jewish fiction from 1880-1930, 1930-1945, and since 1945, respectively. Also pertinent are Section 12, "Images of America in American-Jewish Writing"; Section 13, "Eastern Europe in American-Jewish Writing"; and Section 15, "Fiction of the Holocaust." Each contains a bibliography and suggestions for further reading.

411 Guttman, Allen. *The Jewish Writer in America: Assimilation and the Crisis of Identity.* New York: Oxford University Press, 1971.

A historical and critical study of writers in English from 1654 to the present who treated the subject of assimilation and the crisis of identity which it caused. Special attention is given to Cahan,

Yezierska, Ornitz, Henry Roth, Meyer Levin, Lewisohn, Malamud, and Bellow.

412 Harap, Louis. *Creative Awakening: The Jewish Presence in Twentieth Century American Literature, 1900-1940s.* New York: Greenwood, 1987.

A historical and critical study of the development of the literature, with an emphasis on fiction, including many plot summaries and evaluations. Harap redefines Jewish-American literature as more than that merely concerned with the "theological and traditional aspects." He identifies "American-Jewish first by the identity of the author and second by the ethnic character of the content": it may have "intellectual, environmental, familial, characterological and generational" aspects of Jewishness. Harap explains the historical settings for Jews in American fiction and pays special attention to Cahan, Ornitz, Levin, Michael Gold, Fuchs, and Henry Roth.

413 ————. *In the Mainstream: The Jewish Presence in Twentieth-Century American Literature, 1950s-1980s.* New York: Greenwood, 1987.

A continuation of *Creative Awakening*, with special attention to Bellow and Malamud and secondary attention to Ozick, Potok, and Philip Roth. As the title suggests, these are "mainstream" writers. The book contains a bibliographical note.

414 Malin, Irving, ed. *Contemporary American-Jewish Literature: Critical Essays.* Bloomington: University of Indiana Press, 1973.

Malin uses a "limited" definition of American-Jewish literature: "Only when a Jewish (by birth) writer, moved by religious tensions, shows ultimate concern in creating a new structure of belief...works that invent being a Jew." The essays relevant to immigrant fiction are David Daiches, "Breakthrough"; Allen Guttman, "The Conversion of the Jews"; Melvin J. Friedman, "Jewish Mothers and Sons"; Sheldon Norman Grebstein, "Bernard Malamud and the Jewish Movement"; and Jackson R. Bryer, "Contemporary American-Jewish Literature: A Selected Checklist of Criticism." The emphasis in the collection is on Bellow and Malamud, and the book contains a selected bibliography.

415 Mersand, Joseph. *Traditions in American Literature: A Study of Jewish Characters and Authors.* New York: Modern Chapbooks, 1939. Reprint, Port Washington, NY: Kennikat Press.
One of the earliest works on the subject.

416 Schulz, Max F. *Radical Sophistication: Studies in Contemporary Jewish-American Novelists.* Athens: Ohio University Press, 1969.
Schulz argues that, because of their long history of belief despite uncertainties and doubts, Jewish-American writers bring to their readers a sense of coherence in the midst of the century's chaos.

417 Sherman, Bernard. *The Invention of the Jew: Jewish American Education Novels, 1916-1964.* New York: T. Yoseloff, 1969.
A critical study of some forty novels about growing up Jewish in American cities. The novels are examined chronologically, beginning with Cahan's *The Rise of David Levinsky.*

418 Tuerk, Richard. "Jewish-American Literature." *Ethnic Perspectives in American Literature: Selected Essays on the European Contribution.* Eds. Robert J. Di Pietro and Edward Ifkovic. New York: MLA, 1983.
This critical and historical survey emphasizes those writers who deal with their Jewishness, particularly in prose fiction. It is in this genre, as well as in autobiography, that Jewish-American writers have excelled.

419 Walden, Daniel, ed. *Twentieth Century American Jewish Fiction Writers. Dictionary of Literary Biography,* vol. 28. Detroit: Bruccoli, Clark, 1984.
A collection of biographical and critical introductions to the writers and their fiction.

420 Waxman, Meyer. *A History of Jewish Literature.* New York: Thomas Yoseloff, 1960.
Volume 4, Part 2, and Volume 5 concern American-Jewish fiction written in Yiddish, English, and Hebrew.

421 Wisse, Ruth. *The Schlemiel as Modern Hero.* Chicago: University of Chicago Press, 1971.

Wisse surveys the tradition of the schlemiel (an unlucky and habitual bungler) from Yiddish writer to American-Jewish fiction through the 60s.

KOREAN (see also Asian)

Individual Authors

422 Kang, Younghill. *East Goes West*. New York: Scribner's, 1937. Reprint, Chicago: Follett, 1968.

In this autobiographical novel, the first novel in English by a Korean immigrant, Chungpa Han flees from the Japanese persecution in Korea and comes to the U.S. in 1921. Having made up his mind to stay, he feels isolated from other Korean immigrants who work and give money for Korea's liberation, hoping someday to return. Han attends night-school classes, works as a domestic, a busboy, and a department store clerk, but is never able to find "the land of his dreams." His only friends are other Asians, particularly educated Chinese who can find work only in Chinatown restaurants. When the American woman with whom he falls in love rejects him, he feels lonelier and more disappointed than ever.

423 ———. *The Grass Roof*. New York: Scribner's, 1931.

The story of Chungpa Han's youth in Korea telling the reasons for his departure for the U.S. From an aristocratic family, he had been imprisoned briefly by the Japanese after they annexed Korea in 1909. He chose not to fight with the nationalists, seeing Korea as irrevocably lost, as offering only restrictions to life. Having learned about the U.S. from American missionaries, he set sail just before Asian immigration was cut off, in 1921, with great anticipation for his new and free life.

424 Kim, Ronyoung. *Clay Walls*. Seattle: University of Washington Press, 1990.

When Korea is annexed by Japan in 1910, Chun and Haesu immigrate to Los Angeles, where they must take menial and degrading jobs and are barred from decent housing. Haesu, from an aristocratic family, misses her native land and the "clay walls," which symbolize it. She takes her children back to Korea, but, realizing that they can be no better off there under the Japanese government, returns to the U.S. Things get worse: Chun dies, Haesu must support her children through domestic labor, and American-born son Harold, though a brilliant student, is denied entry to a military academy.

425 Kim, Ruth. *The Family of Chung Song.* New York: Vantage, 1968.

Dong Am, one of the few surviving members of a once prosperous family in Taigu after the Japanese occupation of Korea, wants to go to the U.S. to study medicine. Her Uncle Song Ho, who has worked secretly for United States Intelligence during the war, and has, throughout her life, told her many stories about the customs and behaviors of Americans will help her get there.

426 Pak, Ty. *Guilt Payment.* Honolulu: Bamboo Ridge Press, 1983.

Thirteen stories about the Korean War and post-war immigration to Hawaii.

LEBANESE (see Syrian)

LITHUANIAN

Individual Authors

427 Sinclair, Upton. *The Jungle.* Garden City, NY: Doubleday, Page, 1906.

Although this may be one of the most well-known novels about immigrant life, it is really an exposé of the meatpacking industry at the beginning of the twentieth century and a story of the need for and the growth of the unions. The novel begins with the wedding party of two young Lithuanian immigrants, moves to a flashback of leaving Lithuania and journeying to Chicago, and shows their struggles to achieve some kind of stability in the city. Their lives are harsh in the extreme, because of the lack of cooperation between immigrants, in that all are out for themselves—including the local priest—and the dissolution of the family and the community in the face of the need to struggle for individual survival in a corrupt capitalistic system, like a jungle.

MEXICAN (see also Hispanic)

Individual Authors

428 Acosta, Oscar. *The Autobiography of a Brown Buffalo*. San Francisco: Straight Arrow Press, 1972.

An Oakland lawyer in the 1960s feels culturally rootless and wanders around Idaho, Colorado and Texas and finally goes to Juarez, Mexico to find his identity as a Chicano. Once he does he goes to Los Angeles to help other Chicanos find theirs.

429 ———. *The Revolt of the Cockroach People*. San Francisco: Straight Arrow Press, 1973.

When a Chicano lawyer takes part in a demonstration in 1968 for La Raza and begins to work for the legal defense of its members, his life takes on direction and new meaning.

430 Anaya, Rudolfo. *Bless Me, Última*. Berkeley: Quinto Sol, 1972. Houston: Arte Publico, 1986.

Antonio Marez comes of age in the 1940s in a remote village in northern New Mexico. The harshness of life and the deaths of those around him lead him to question the Catholic faith of his mother's family, but a wise old woman, who is considered a healer by some and a witch by others, teaches him that he can be both pantheist and Christian, spiritual healer and free spirit.

431 ———. *Heart of Aztlán*. Berkeley, CA: Editorial Justa, 1976.

Clemente and Adelita Chavez must leave their rural community near Guadalupe and move to a barrio in Albuquerque, where the family have trouble adjusting to the crowded and ugly urban environment. Clemente drinks too much; the youngest son becomes addicted to drugs; and the daughters drop out of school and reject their Chicano identity. What saves them is the determination of Adelita and the second son, Jason, to hold the family together, as well as the inspiration of a blind poet, Crispin, who urges Clemente to change his life and be a leader of the Chicanos in the barrio.

432 ———. *The Silence of the Llano*. Houston: Arte Publico, 1982.

A collection of short stories (in addition to three excerpts from his novels) about Chicanos in New Mexico.

433 Arias, Ron. *The Road to Tamazunchale*. Reno, NV: West Coast Poetry Review Press, 1975. Reprint, Ypsilanti, MI: Bilingual Press, 1987.

Written in the tradition of the modern Latin American novel of magic realism, this is the story of Fausto Tejada, a retired bookseller in a Los Angeles Chicano community. As he is dying, he dreams of the past and of a journey to Cuzco, Peru, home of the ancient Incan civilization, while he also remembers the illegal immigrants whom he had sheltered from the police.

434 Barrio, Raymond. *The Plum Plum Pickers*. New York: Canfield, 1971.

The story of Manuel Guiterrez and his wife Lupe, farm laborers in the Santa Clara Valley in California, who live in shacks and work dawn to dusk, yet are in debt to the company store. Finally fed up, Manuel rallies the other workers around him against the middleman contractor Roberto Morales, who cheats his own people to get ahead and impress the Anglo farm owner.

435 Brawley, Ernest. *Selena*. New York: Atheneum, 1979. Reprint, New York: Simon and Schuster, 1984.

A young woman takes the side of her people in organizing strikes against the owner of the farm, an ex-lover.

436 Candelaria, Nash. *Memories of the Alhambra*. Palo Alto, CA: Cibola Press, 1977.

José Rafa, son of a successful businessman in Los Angeles, searches for his cultural roots, first in Mexico, where he denies any Indian ancestry, and then in Spain, where he wants to affirm a pure Spanish ancestry, because it is more socially acceptable. His son assimilates to Anglo culture and marries an Anglo woman.

437 Chávez, Denise. *The Last of the Menu Girls*. Houston: Arte Publico, 1986.

Seven connected narratives about Rocio, who rebels against her society's expectations of young women by wanting to become a writer. In her first summer job as a hospital aide in New Mexico, she brings menus to the patients, both Chicano and Anglo, and she gets emotionally involved with them. After a traffic accident, she returns to the hospital as a patient and discovers that there are no longer any menu girls.

438   Chávez, Fray Angelico. *From an Altar Screen, El Retablo: Tales from New Mexico*. Freeport, NY: Books for Libraries Series, 1943.

A Franciscan priest's collection of stories that utilize the folklore and local color of New Mexico and its Chicano residents and deal mainly with religious themes.

439   ———. *New Mexico Triptych*. Sante Fe, NM: William Gannon, 1976.

More stories in the same vein as in the other collection.

440   Cisneros, Sandra. *The House on Mango Street*. Houston: Arte Publico, 1984. Reprint, New York: Random House, 1991.

A series of vignettes told by Esperanza Cordero, who wants to be a writer, growing up in a poor Hispanic neighborhood in Chicago in the 1970s, about her own experiences and those of her neighbors, particularly girls and women. The book won the Before Columbus American Book Award in 1985.

441   ———. *Woman Hollering Creek and Other Stories*. New York: Random House, 1991.

Stories about life on the San Antonio-Mexican border, with a focus on women's experiences: some are vignettes like those of her earlier book; a few are longer stories.

442   Fernández, Roberta. *Intaglio: A Novel in Six Stories*. Houston: Arte Publico, 1990.

Each story focuses on a woman living on the Rio Grande border, and the whole reflects on how women's culture was passed down from the older generation to the younger.

443   Galarza, Ernesto. *Barrio Boy*. South Bend, IN: Notre Dame University Press, 1971.

An autobiographical novel about a boy's move with his family from a mountain village in central Mexico to a barrio in California and his gradual difficult assimilation to U.S. culture through school. The story ends with his working in a migrant camp and being fired for trying to organize the laborers.

444   García, Lionel G. *A Shroud in the Family*. Houston: Arte Publico, 1987.

A large Chicano family struggles with Anglo culture in Houston, but the protagonist is able to debunk the myths about the supposed Anglo heroes who fought to make Texas part of the U.S.

445 González, Genaro. *Only Sons*. Houston: Arte Publico, 1991.
A collection of seven stories about father-son relationships on the Texas-Mexico border, focusing particularly on the tradition of "machismo," which leads to problems within the family.

446 ———. *Rainbow's End*. Houston: Arte Publico, 1988.
A three-generation novel beginning with the grandfather, who swam across the Rio Grande River. The family, living in the Lower Rio Grande Valley of Texas, are forced to become migrant laborers. To make enough money to live on, they become drug smugglers.

447 Hernández, Irene Beltram. *Across the Great River*. Houston: Arte Publico, 1989.
As seen from the point of view of a young girl, the story of a family's illegal entry into the United States and their experiences with labor smugglers, rape and other violence.

448 Hinojosa, Rolando. *Becky and Her Friends*. Houston: Arte Publico, 1989.
This, the most recent of the Klail City novels, focuses on women and particularly Becky Escobar and her rebellion against the dominance of men and the church.

449 ———. *Dear Rafe*. Houston: Arte Publico, 1985.
The third of the Klail City novels. The first part is a collection of letters written between Jehu Malacara, who works at a bank, to his friend Rafe Buenrostro. The letters tell of Malacara's dissatisfaction with his job and the Anglos who control the valley, and end with his leaving town to attend the University of Texas. The second part is a series of interviews with the valley residents who are described in the letters.

450 ———. *Fair Gentlemen of Belken County*. Houston: Arte Publico, 1986.
The sixth in the Klail City series. Malacara and Buenrostro are

featured again, but its setting is prior to that of *Rites and Witnesses*. Buenrostro and Malacara both serve in the army during the Korean War. The book focuses on a character who appeared as a principal character in the first two of the series: Estaban Echeverria, the oldest man in the valley, who recounts stories of the residents of and the events and changes that have occurred in Belken County.

451 ———. *Klail City.* 1977. Translated by Rosaura Sanchez. Houston: Arte Publico Press, 1987.

The second of the Klail City novels. Some of the characters from the first novel reappear, notably Rafe Buenrostro and Jehu Malacara, but the lives of over a hundred characters in the community, past and present, are seen as connected. As in *Sketches of the Valley*, the stories are presented in a variety of ways and not in any chronological order.

452 ———. *Partners in Crime: A Rafe Buenrostro Mystery.* Houston: Arte Publico Press, 1985.

The fifth in the Klail City series, this novel continues the story of Malacara, who, having finished graduate school, is the vice-president of Klail City First National Bank, and of Buenrostro, a law school graduate, who is a lieutenant of the Belken County homicide squad. Together they investigate murders that are a result of an invasion in their county by multi-national corporations and crime syndicates.

453 ———. *Rites and Witnesses.* Houston: Arte Publico Press, 1982.

This fourth in the series of Klail City novels consists of stories, dialogues, commentaries, and documents (fifty-one of them). Set just prior to *Dear Rafe*, it tells of the first daily encounters of Jehu Malacara and Rafe Buenrostro with the Anglo world: the former as the first Chicano to work at a Klail City bank; the latter as a returning wounded veteran from Korea.

454 ———. *Sketches of the Valley.* Berkeley, CA: Quinto Sol, 1973. Reprint, Ypsilanti, MI: Bilingual Press, 1983, translation by Gustavo Valadez.

The first in his series of novels about Mexican-American life in the fictional south Texas Belken County. Set from the 1930s through the 1950s, it is a collection of interrelated sketches about the inhabitants of the valley, either narrated alternately by the omniscient author and two characters—Jehu Malacara and Rafe Buenrostro—or presented as conversations, documents, and commentaries. Together they present a panorama of daily life in the community, as the Chicanos live among the Anglos, yet hold dear their own values and traditions.

455 Islas, Arturo. *Migrant Souls.* New York: Morrow, 1990.
A Chicano family living near the Mexican border in New Mexico are proud of both their cultures and are happy to be U.S. citizens, although they have to carry identification papers, and the children are still called aliens at school and are puzzled by the Anglo and New England bent of their holidays. Crossing the border into Mexico is an easy process, but returning to the U.S. requires questioning and humiliation.

456 ———. *The Rain God: A Desert Tale.* Houston: Arte Publico, 1984.
Six connected stories told by an omniscient narrator in the style of magic realism about three generations of the Angel family of El Paso, focusing on the grandson Miguel Chico, a writer, and his attempts to identify with his Mexican past and the ancient religion.

457 Keller, Gary D. [El Huitlacoche]. *Tales of El Huitlacoche.* Houston: Arte Publico, 1984.
Four humorous stories satirizing U.S. society. "Papi Invented the Automatic Jumping Bean" concerns a man who attempts to educate his sons through getting rich by his invention, but his secret is discovered and marketed by Anglos. "Mocha in Disneyland" is about a professor, divorced from his Anglo wife, who tells his son myths about the origin of the Chicano people.

458 Martínez, Max. *The Adventures of the Chicano Kid and Other Stories.* Houston: Arte Publico, 1982.
Accounts of Chicano life in the small towns and big cities of Texas. The title story is a parody of nineteenth century "dime novels," in which the traditional roles of Anglos and Chicanos are reversed, and the Chicano Kid is the hero. Another story "Dona Petra" concerns the revenge of a woman on the Texas Rangers, who have killed both her husband and her son.

459 Morales, Alejandro. *The Brick People*. Houston: Arte Publico, 1991.

A historical novel which traces the growth of California in the nineteenth and twentieth centuries, through a focus on the Simons brick factory and its immigrant workers.

460 Portillo, Estela Trambley. *Rain of Scorpions and Other Writings*. Berkeley, CA: Tonatiuh International, 1975.

The title story is set in a small mining town near El Paso, in which Fito, a handicapped Vietnam War veteran, tries to organize the townspeople to confront the social oppression and environmental exploitation of the Anglo mine owners. He is then aided in his attempt to begin a new life with a Mother Earth figure called Lupe. All of the stories have a feminist focus.

461 ———. *Trini*. Houston: Arte Publico, 1986.

A Tarahumara woman crosses the border without papers to give birth to her child in the U.S. and to fulfill her dream of owning her own land. With both goals accomplished, she plans to return to Mexico with her children to acquaint them with their traditions and culture.

462 Ríos, Alberto Alvaro. *The Iguana Killer: Twelve Stories of the Heart*. Lewiston, ID: Blue Moon and Confluence, 1984.

For young adults. Most of the stories deal with the rites of growing up. In the title story, a Mexican boy visits his grandmother in Arizona and sees his first snow and baseball bat, which seems to him an apt weapon for killing iguanas.

463 Rivera, Tomás. *This Migrant Earth*. Translated by Rolando Hinojosa. Houston: Arte Publico, 1987.

Rivera's novel, originally published in 1971 in a bilingual edition, with an English translation by Herminio Rios, entitled *And the Earth Did Not Part*, consists of twelve connected stories about a group of migrant workers as they follow the crops from south Texas to the northern Midwest. They are told through descriptive passages and dialogues as well as the prayers, thoughts, reflections and memories of the characters, particularly the unnamed boy who is the main character.

464 Soto, Gary. *Living up the Street.* San Francisco: Strawberry Hill, 1985.

For young adults. Twenty-one autobiographical stories about a boy growing up in the barrio of Fresno, California. "Black Hair" concerns the boy at seventeen, who has run away and taken a job in a factory, where, working mainly with blacks and illegal Mexicans, he comes to sympathize with the uncertain and dangerous life of undocumented aliens. This book won the 1985 American Book Award.

465 Valdéz, Gina. *There Are No Madmen Here.* Houston: Arte Publico, 1981.

Three short stories and an autobiographical novel, *Maria Portillo.* The stories are about immigrant Maria's daughter, father, and brother, respectively. The novel is about Maria's struggle, after she is abandoned by her husband, to support herself and her three children in Los Angeles, with the help of her extended family in both the U.S. and Mexico, and about her realization that her children have been radically influenced by growing up in an Anglo culture.

466 Vásquez, Richard. *Chicano.* New York: Doubleday, 1970.

A three-generation novel, beginning with a couple who escape the devastation of war in their village in Mexico and ride a boxcar to the U.S. One of their sons becomes a successful engineer in Los Angeles, but is not accepted in the suburban Anglo community to which he moves. His daughter gets involved romantically with an Anglo, who rejects her when she is pregnant.

467 Villareal, José A. *Clemente Chacón.* Binghamton, NY: Bilingual Press, 1984.

A boy born and raised on the Mexican side of the border comes alone as an adolescent to the U.S. He becomes an executive in an insurance company but comes into conflict with his ambition and La Raza, a group of union organizers.

468 ———. *Pocho.* New York: Anchor Books, 1970.

Juan Rubio, a Mexican revolutionary, kills a rich Spaniard and must flee across the border to California, where his wife and children later join him. But their disillusionment with the Anglo church and the problems of unemployment bring about the dissolution of the family. Juan leaves his wife, the oldest daughter Luz marries an Anglo, and the son Richard leaves home to join the navy.

469 Villasenor, Edmund. *Macho.* New York: Bantam, 1973. Reprint, Houston: Arte Publico Press, 1991.

Seventeen-year-old Roberto Garcia leaves the state of Michoacan and enters the U.S. illegally. He is cheated by his Mexican labor contractor, who had promised to get him legal status. While working at back-breaking farm work for long hours with low pay, he is determined to prove his *machismo* and to rise above his fellows. He robs and cheats the other laborers and works as a strike breaker, and eventually he makes a lot of money.

470 ———. *Rain of Gold.* Houston: Arte Publico, 1991.

Autobiographical narratives about the author's family, how they came to California after the Mexican Revolution of 1910 and settled in there.

471 Viramontes, Helena María *The Moths and Other Stories.* Houston: Arte Publico, 1985.

Eight short stories focusing on women of all ages. The title story concerns a teenage girl who resists giving in to her male- and church-dominated society. When her grandmother, the only one who understands and approves of her, dies, the girl grieves, not only for her, but for herself as she faces an oppressive womanhood.

Anthologies

472 Anaya, Rudolfo and Antonio Marquez, eds. *Cuentos Chicanos: A Short Story Anthology.* Albuquerque: University of New Mexico Press, 1984.

Twenty-one stories, mostly in English and by established writers.

473 De Dwyer, Carlota Cárdenas, ed. *Chicano Voices.* Boston: Houghton Mifflin, 1975.

Contains poetry, a play, and essays in addition to fiction by José Villareal, Floyd Salas, Raymond Barrio, Edmund Villasenor,

Américo Paredes, John Rechy, Tomás Rivera, and Richard Vásquez—writings mainly from the 1960s and 1970s.

474 Gonzalez, Ray, ed. *Mirrors Beneath the Earth.* Willimantic, CT: Curbstone Press, 1992.

Thirty-one short stories by young writers—some established, some published for the first time or for the first time in an anthology. Their works share two important aspects: "real knowledge of the world and wild, imaginary adventures grounded in family myths, superstition, and traditional values."

475 Hart, Dorothy E. and Lewis M. Baldwin, eds. *Voices of Aztlán: Chicano Literature of Today.* New York: National American Library, 1974.

A selection including poetry and drama, but also short stories and excerpts from novels.

476 Lopez, Tiffany Ana, ed. *Growing Up Chicana/Chicano: An Anthology.* New York: Morrow, 1993.

Twenty stories, mostly by established writers, in four sections: One includes stories about traveling over the border; Two, those concerned with learning from grandparents; Three, stories about school; and Four, about "passages" to adulthood.

477 Ortega, Phillip D., ed. *We Are Chicanos: An Anthology of Mexican-American Literature.* New York: Washington Square Press, 1973.

In the introduction, Ortega traces the roots of Chicano literature and claims to include a "wide and varied selection" of background history, folklore, poetry, drama and fiction.

478 Paredes, Américo and Raymund Paredes, eds. *Mexican-American Authors.* Boston: Houghton Mifflin, 1972.

Short stories, essays and poems—all translated from Spanish; the book is meant to be a textbook for beginning students.

479 Salinas, Luis Omar and Lillian Faderman, eds. *From the Barrio: A Chicano Anthology.* San Francisco: Canfield, 1973.

Includes fiction by Américo Paredes, Richard Vásquez, Rudy Gallardo, José Villareal, Juan Garcia and Nick C. Vaca.

480 Simmen, Edward, ed. *The Chicanos: From Caricature to Self-Portrait.* New York: New American Library, 1971.
Short stories by Anglo writers about Chicanos at work and by Chicano authors.

481 ———. *North of the Rio Grande: The Mexican-American Experience in Short Fiction.* New York: Penguin, 1992.
A collection of thirty-five stories set from the late nineteenth century to the present by a variety of writers, both Anglo and Chicano, providing a dual perspective into the two cultures living side by side.

Secondary Sources

482 Bruce-Novoa, Juan D., ed. *Chicano Authors: Inquiry by Interview.* Austin: University of Texas Press, 1980.
Interviews with major Chicano authors: Anaya, Hinojosa, Portillo, Villareal and others. Each interview is preceded by a biographical note. The introduction to the section on fiction emphasizes the theme of family as it is being subjected to fragmentary social pressures.

483 ———. *Retrospace: Collected Essays on Chicano Literature.* Houston: Arte Publico, 1990.
Fifteen critical essays which "treat history and/or the historical aspects of the literature" and assert that immigration and deculturation are favorite subjects of the novelists.

484 Calderon, Hector and José David Saldivar, eds. *Criticism in the Borderlands: Studies in Chicano Literature, Culture, and Idealogy.* Durham, N.C.: Duke University Press, 1991.
Aside from critical essays, the editors include a briefly annotated bibliography of contemporary Chicano literature, compiled by Roberto Trujillo.

485 García-Giron, Edmondo. "The Chicanos: An Overview." *Ethnic Literatures Since 1776: The Many Voices of America.* Eds. Wolodymyr T. Zyla and Wendall M. Aycock. Lubbock: Proceedings of the Comparative Literature Symposium, Texas Tech University, Jan. 1976.
Traces the history of Chicano literature from its Indian roots

and discusses some genres, figures and trends from the 1950s.

486 Herrara-Sobek, María, ed. *Beyond Stereotypes: The Critical Analysis of Chicana Literature*. Binghamton, NY: Bilingual Press, 1985.
Includes four essays on the fiction of women writers and the treatment of Chicanas in literature.

487 Lattin, Vernon E. *Contemporary Chicano Fiction: A Critical Survey*. Binghamton, NY: Bilingual Press, 1986.
Twenty-six essays on Villareal, Barrio, Hinojosa, Anaya and others. Contains a selected bibliography of criticism compiled by Ernestina N. Eger.

488 Lewis, Marvin A. *Introduction to the Chicano Novel*. Milwaukee: University of Milwaukee Press, 1982.
A culturalist approach to works by leading novelists.

489 Lomelí, Francisco A. and Carl R. Shirley, eds. *Chicano Writers, First Series. Dictionary of Literary Biography*, vol. 82. Detroit: Bruccoli Clark, Layman Books, 1989.
Biographical and critical introductions to fifty-two writers.

490 ———. Chicano *Writers, Second Series. Dictionary of Literary Biography*, vol. 122. Detroit: Bruccoli Clark, Layman Books, 1992.
Biographical and critical introductions to sixty-four writers.

491 Martínez, Julio A., and Francisco A. Lomelí. *Chicano Literature: A Reference Guide*. Westport, CT: Greenwood, 1985.
Short critical and biographical essays, with bibliographies of individual authors and a general bibliography.

492 Paredes, Raymund A. "The Evolution of Chicano Literature." *MELUS* 5:2 (Summer, 1978), 71-110.
A historical and critical survey, with a definition of Chicano literature, leading to a discussion of fiction written in English.

493 Robinson, Cecil. *With the Ears of Strangers: The Mexican in American Literature*. Tucson: University of Arizona Press, 1963.
A historical study of how Mexicans and Mexican-Americans

have been portrayed in poetry and fiction written by non-Mexicans: from derogatory to romanticized stereotypes.

494 Saldivar, Ramon. *Chicano Narrative: The Dialectics of Difference.* Madison: University of Wisconsin Press, 1990.

A theoretical perspective on fiction, with special attention to Villareal, Anaya, Hinojosa, and Cisneros. He asserts that "Chicano narrative should be seen as an active participant in [the] reconceptualization of American literary discourse" and that Chicano authors attempt to "fashion. . . a new, heterogeneous American consciousness within the dialectics of difference."

495 Shirley, Carl R. and Paula W. *Understanding Chicano Literature.* Columbia: University of South Carolina Press, 1988.

One of the "Understanding Contemporary American Literature" series, this is a survey which is meant to be a primer, especially for Anglo students. Chapter Three deals with the novel, and Chapter Four with the short story. The book contains a suggested reading list and bibliography.

496 Tatum, Charles. *Chicano Literature.* Boston: Twayne, 1982.

The first book-length study in English of Chicano literature, this is an introduction to the poetry, drama, and fiction. Beginning with a historical background and an explanation of bilingualism in Chicano literature or "code switching," it moves to studies of individual genres, with chapters on the contemporary Chicano short story and novel. It includes a selected bibliography of both primary and secondary sources, with brief annotations.

497 Vallejos, Thomas. "Ritual Process and the Family in the Chicano Novel." *MELUS* 10:4 (Winter, 1983), 5-17.

Proposes that the Chicano novel is often interpreted as a transition between cultures but should also be appreciated, if appropriate, as an affirmation of traditional family and community values.

Bibliographies

498 Eger, Ernestina N., compiler. *A Bibliography of Criticism of Contemporary Chicano Literature.* Monograph 5. Berkeley, CA: Chicano Studies Library, 1982.

Over 1,000 entries, mainly of works published after 1960.

499 Lomelí, Francisco A., and Donaldo W. Urioste, compilers. *Chicano Perspectives in Literature: A Critical and Annotated Bibliography.* Albuquerque: Pajarito, 1976.

500 McKenna, Teresa, compiler. "Chicano Literature: A Bibliography." *Redefining American Literary History.* Eds. A. LaVonne Brown Ruoff and Jerry W. Ward, Jr. New York: MLA, 1990.
Contains brief annotations about bibliographies, anthologies, oral literature, and primary and secondary works.

NORWEGIAN (see also Scandinavian)

Individual Authors

501 Bojer, Johan. *The Emigrants.* Translated by A. G. Jayne. New York: Century, 1925. Reprint, New York: Atheneum, 1974.
A group gather under the leadership of Erik Foss, a returned settler, and set out to be pioneers in the Red River Valley in North Dakota. The parents intend to save money so that they can go back to Norway, but the American-born children see themselves as American and want to stay.

502 Boyeson, Hjalmar H. *Falconberg.* New York: Scribner's, 1899.
The novel opens with the narrator's satirical description of the superior attitude of the Nordic immigrants—in their dignity, morality and temperament—coming through Castle Garden in the 1870s and goes on to tell the tale of one of them. The young wastral, Einar Falconberg, flees to America after forging his father's name on a check. In Minnesota he changes his name to Finnson and joins an established and growing Norwegian settlement. He becomes a journalist and incurs the wrath of a powerful branch of the Norwegian-American church for espousing a liberal political party in his newspaper. The bishop has learned of his boyhood crime and publicly denounces Einar; but the woman he loves, Helga, and some other townspeople forgive and support him. He and Helga marry and become happily assimilated Americans.

503 Dahl, Borghild. *Homecoming.* New York: Dutton, 1953.

Lyng Skoglund grows up in a strict immigrant household in Minneapolis and resents feeling like a foreigner at school. Wanting very much to be like other Americans, she goes to the state university rather than to her church college to be an English teacher, but the only position she can get, after earning her degree, is in a small conservative Norwegian town in northwest Minnesota. Though she is initially disappointed, through the school year she comes to accept and be proud of her Norwegian heritage, while at the same time she is able to impress upon her students and the townspeople the advantages of an American education.

504 ———. *Karen.* New York: Dutton, 1947.

Realizing that she and her younger sister have poor prospects for a future on the family farm in Norway, Karen shepherds Swanhild to America and through Castle Garden on their way to Dubuque, Iowa to join their brother and to work as domestic servants. Karen is respected for her industry and thoroughness. Eventually both women marry and have their own households, Karen as a homesteader in Dakota territory.

505 Forbes, Kathryn. *Mama's Bank Account.* New York: Harcourt, Brace, 1943.

Katrin tells stories about growing up with her mama and papa, aunts and uncles on Castro Street in San Francisco, the only Norwegians in that area. Though the immigrants have become naturalized citizens and embrace American life, they also consider themselves Norwegian and are proud of those customs and values as well. The play *I Remember Mama* is based on this book and its sequels.

506 Matson, Norman. *Day of Fortune.* New York: Century, 1928.

An immigrant has difficulty keeping jobs and moves from one city to another, so that his children feel rootless. When their mother dies, they disperse, losing quickly all sense of ethnicity.

507 Peterson, James A. *Solstad: The Old and the New.* Minneapolis: Augsburg, 1923.

Arne, a peasant orphan, proposes to his landowner's daughter in Norway, but, rejected, goes to America to make his fortune. He returns to Norway with sufficient money to impress the father and is allowed to marry the woman. When her father visits them in the U.S., he is so further impressed that he too builds a home on the prairie and becomes an American citizen.

508 Rölvaag, O. E. *The Boat of Longing*. New York: Harper and Brothers, 1921. Reprint, Westport, CT, Greenwood, 1974.

Nils Vaag immigrates to America and writes enthusiastic letters home to his parents, until he falls upon hard times, and his parents no longer hear from him. His father sails to America to find him but is turned back at Ellis Island. Home in Norway, he makes up a story about Nils' success to tell his wife.

509 ———. *Giants in the Earth*. Translated by the author and Lincoln Colcord. New York: Harper and Brothers, 1927. Reprint, New York: Harper and Row, 1966.

This story of immigrant life on the prairie has become a classic of American literature. Per Hansa takes his wife Beret and their children by ship through Canada and then overland by oxcart to a homestead in Dakota Territory in the 1870s. He is delighted with owning his own farm and making it prosper; but she keenly misses her parents and the community and church of her native village. She fears the prairie and what she imagines are its demons, suffering a breakdown after she gives birth to their fourth child. Becoming religiously fanatic, she shames her husband into attempting to bring a minister for their dying friend, Hans Olsa, during a blizzard.

510 ———. *Peder Victorious*. Translated by the author and Nora O. Solum. New York: Harper and Brothers, 1929.

The sequel to *Giants*. Beret's youngest son begins to lose his faith when he learns how his father died. As he grows to manhood he has conflicts with the strictures of his Norwegian church. He wants to go to public—not parochial—school, to take part in school activities—like plays—that his pastor disapproves of, and to date Susie, who is Irish and Catholic. Beret, like the pastor, is dismayed at Peder's moving away from his ethnic values; but, remembering her own unconventional behavior with Per Hansa, finally gives her son her approval.

511 ————. *Pure Gold*. Translated by the author and Sivert Erdahl. New York: Harper and Brothers, 1930.

Just before and during World War I, prompted by the nativist movement, a second generation couple, Lars and Lizzie Houglum, drop all aspects of their Norwegian culture to be totally American: for instance, Lars becomes Louis, and they discontinue their church attendance and their subscription to a Norwegian newspaper. Their main interest is in how much money they can make and save. Eventually their greed and ambition consume them.

512 ————. *Their Father's God*. Translated by Trygve M. Ager. New York: Harper and Brothers, 1931. Reprint, Lincoln: University of Nebraska Press, 1983.

The last novel in the Per Hansa and Beret trilogy, it traces the breakdown of Peder's marriage to Susie and treats the problems of mixed marriages, the tension between building a new life in a new world, and the importance of family traditions. Susie takes their son and leaves Peder.

513 Rud, Anthony M. *The Second Generation*. Garden City, NY: Doubleday, Page, 1923.

Einar Merssen sneaks out of Norway when his girlfriend becomes pregnant and his father will not give him money or stock to start his own farm. Some years later, his son Lief comes to the U.S. to find his father. But Einar, who has married another woman, treats him brutally. Lief runs away from home, and assisted by a doctor friend, is able to attend medical school and become a doctor. When he marries and has a son, he vows to give the boy all the advantages he himself had never had.

514 Shank, Margarethe Erdahl. *The Coffee Train*. Garden City, NY: Doubleday, 1954. Reprint, 1968.

Written from the point of view of a girl who grows up in the Norwegian community of a North Dakota town in the 1920s. Her mother had died in childbirth, a result, her immigrant grandparents tell her, of her father's having been "too ardent," and her father had left the family. Magrit tells vignettes of her eccentric bachelor uncle and her beautiful aunt Gudrun, who is in love with a divorced man. Norwegian is the language spoken at home, but all the uncles and aunts go to college. Gudrun sits on the draft board during World War I and is the first woman from that area to run for public office after the war.

515 Young, Carrie. *The Wedding Dress: Stories from the Dakota Plains.* Iowa City: University of Iowa Press, 1992.
Seven stories about growing up in a Norwegian farm community in the 1920s and 1930s.

POLISH (see also Slavic)

Individual Authors

516 Algren, Nelson. *The Neon Wilderness.* Garden City, NY: Doubleday, 1947. Reprint, Magnolia, MA: Peter Smith, 1969.
A collection of short stories about the hard lives of Polish immigrants and their children in a tough neighborhood on Chicago's West Side.

517 Bankowsky, Richard. *A Glass Rose.* New York: Random House, 1958.
A stream-of-consciousness novel from the points of view of the attendants at the wake of Stanislaw Machek, who came to the U.S. with his wife, Rozalja, and his friends Jozef and Pyotr to escape conscription in the Austrian army and the hopelessness of earning a decent living on their small, worthless farms. They settle in New Jersey, close to the factory in which the men work. A violent strike that causes Stanislaw's injury and the deaths of several of their children lead to Rozalja's madness, the disintegration of the family, and Stanislaw's alcoholism and suicide.

518 Krawczyk, Monica. *If the Branch Blossoms and Other Stories.* Minneapolis: Polonie, 1950.
Stories from a woman's viewpoint, which describe the struggles of poor immigrant families in Minneapolis and environs. The women must play the traditional, subservient roles, while producing and caring for many children and working hard in the home or at domestic labor for others. Their husbands are drunk and uncooperative at the worst, or hard-working but unsympathetic at best.

519 Kubiac, Wanda Luzenska. *Polonaise Nevermore*. New York: Vantage, 1962.

Polish immigrants come to Berlin, Wisconsin, between 1866 and 1890 to farm, but they find that they are not entirely welcome to the earlier English and German settlers. Mistreated at the parish church, they join together to build a Polish church and hope to bring there a priest who will conduct services in Polish.

520 Lampell, Millard. *The Hero*. New York: J. Nessner, 1949.

Steve Novak, the son of immigrants in White Falls, a New Jersey milltown, gets a four-year athletic scholarship to a small, prestigious college in Virginia. There, because of his dress and his Catholic religion, he feels awkward among the Protestant and Anglo-Saxon students; but when he goes home to visit, he finds that he is also out of place in the Polish community.

521 Rodman, Maia Wojciechowska. *Till the Break of Day*. New York: Harcourt Brace Jovanovich, 1972.

A refugee from World War II, the daughter of a Polish Air Force Officer, looks back on her girlhood in Cracow before it was bombed and her episodes in France, Lisbon, and London, as she, her mother, and her brother flee the Nazis. Eventually they are allowed to immigrate to the U.S.

522 Tabrah, Ruth. *Pulaski Place*. New York: Harper and Brothers, 1950.

Steve Kowalski returns to Milltown after serving in the army in World War II, deciding that he wants a life different from that of his father, who still lives in the house where he was born the year after his parents arrived from Poland, and still works at the factory where his father had worked. Steve overcomes the prejudice of the city officials in becoming the town's first policeman of Polish descent, but angers his old friends and his relatives when he refuses to bend the law in their favor. Feeling alienated from his community, he and his wife Irene move out of the neighborhood and the parish church. After his brother is killed in a car crash, Steve realizes that he needs his family and community ties and returns to live in his old neighborhood.

523 Vogel, Joseph. *Man's Courage*. New York: Knopf, 1938. Reprint, Syracuse, NY: Syracuse University Press, 1989.

Polish immigrant Adam Wolak tries to own his own land in "Genesee" (Utica), New York. Though he is strong and moral and has a firm trust in American ideals, he is consistently thwarted by bureaucrats and ward politicians. The hundreds of the poor and unemployed who come to his funeral frighten those officials, who realize that they will have trouble holding on to their power.

524 Zebrowski, John. *Uncle Bruno.* San Juan, P.R: Janus, 1972.

Humorous stories of an impetuous and impulsive man, including his escape from Poland to the U.S. after attacking a Russian army officer, his attempts to marry a rich widow, and his presiding at a Christmas Eve party though he claims to be an atheist.

Anthologies

525 Morska, Irene, ed. *Polish Authors of Today and Yesterday.* New York: S. F. Vanni, 1947.

Most of these stories are translated from Polish and are about the oppression of the Poles by various neighboring conquerors; the stories, thereby, provide insights into the reasons for the large immigration of Poles to the U.S. Stories originally written in English by Polish-Americans are the following: Ed Falkowski, "Our Father and We" about a fifteen-year-old boy who comes to Pennsylvania and works for 30 years as a miner, taking part in the unionization of various ethnic workers, and of his son, who visits Poland but is happy to return to his real home, the U.S.; Sydor Rey, "The General," about an American citizen who returns to his Polish village in his American Army uniform for a visit and is considered a hero for standing up to the landlord's overseer; and Irene Morska, "The Chains," a reminiscence about a period spent in a Polish jail as a political prisoner before her immigration to the U.S.

Secondary Sources

526 Maciuszko, Jerzy J. "Polish-American Literature." *Ethnic Perspectives in American Literature: Selected Essays on the European Contribution.* Eds. Robert J. Di Pietro and Edward Ifkovic. New York: MLA, 1983.

A historical overview of several genres. The emphasis is on

works published in the U.S. by Polish-American authors, though not all in English and not all to do with the immigrant experience. It includes a section on the image of Poles in American fiction by non-Poles.

527 Wrobel, Paul. "The Polish American Experience: An Anthropological View of Ruth Tabrah's *Pulaski Place* and Millard Lampell's *The Hero.*" *Ethnic Literatures Since 1776: The Many Voices of America.* Eds. Wolodymyr T. Zyla and Wendall M. Aycock. Lubbock: Proceedings of the Comparative Literature Symposium, Texas Tech Univ., Jan. 1976. IX (1978) II, 395-407.

   The discussion suggests that there is little Polish-American literature so identified, because Polish-Americans have been discouraged from writing about themselves and their communities by a society which rewards assimilation and encourages homogeneity. A definition of Polish-American fiction is tentatively set forth and these two novels are discussed in that context.

PORTUGUESE

Individual Authors

528 Lewis [Luiz], Alfred. *Home Is an Island.* New York: Random House, 1957.

   Juan de Castro's father had been to America via a whaling vessel, had mined for gold in California, and returned home to the Azores, poor but full of adventure stories and determined that his son should make his fortune in the U.S. Many other men have returned with such souvenirs as denim shirts and phonographs and with stories of their good salaries from sheepherding and construction work. Juan's mother wants him to stay home and become a priest. Juan studies hard and leans first one way, then another. When World War I begins, Juan borrows two hundred dollars and sets sail for the United States, simultaneously excited and sad to leave his family, teacher, priest and girlfriend.

529 Oaktree [Carvalho], James. *Haole Come Back!* Chicago: Adams, 1975.

   A Portuguese family, immigrants to Hawaii, go to an isolated place in the mountains when their neighbors force them to move.

530 Roll, Elvira Osorio. *Hawaii's Kohala Breezes*. New York: Exposition Press, 1964.

Young Infelice Damus is the daughter of an immigrant shopkeeper and a genteel mother from Madeira, who considers herself superior both to the working class Portuguese in Hawaii and to the native Hawaiians. Infelice and her sisters are sent to convent schools to learn English and French and be educated as proper Europeans. But then, Infelice, for her part, is hurt by the superior attitude of the Anglo upper classes, who call her "Porgee," even after she marries plantation owner Jack Walker. She comes to be a firm and outspoken believer in the American ideal, using a housewife's metaphor for the "melting pot": the American "cake," in which diverse ingredients make something that should be pleasing to all.

Secondary Sources

531 Baden, Nancy. "Portuguese-American Literature: Does it Exist?" *MELUS* 6:2 (Summer, 1979), 15-31.

Baden suggests that, even if, according to most views, there is none, a "young immigrant literature" does exist, and more works will be forthcoming.

532 Pap, Leo. "Portuguese-American Literature." *Ethnic Perspectives in American Literature: Selected Essays on the European Contribution*. Eds. Robert J. Di Pietro and Edward Ifkovic. New York: MLA, 1983.

Pap comments that the published literature has been "modest so far" because this immigrant group has been limited in numbers and educational opportunities. Of that which exists, most are travel accounts and autobiographies, and most are written in Portuguese. Of English language novels, he mentions, with little comment, those of Luiz, Roll, and Carvalho.

533 Rogers, Francis H. "The Contribution by Americans of Portuguese Descent to the U.S. Literary Scene." *Ethnic Literatures Since 1776: The Many Voices of America*. Eds. Wolodymyr T. Zyla and Wendall Aycock. Lubbock: Proceedings of the Comparative Literature Symposium, Texas Tech University, Jan. 1976. IX (1978) I, 409-432.

A survey of Portuguese-American literature, in both

Portuguese and English, leading to a discussion of the novels of Luiz, Carvalho, and Roll, whose contributions are the greatest. Rogers comments that most of the literature is from Hawaii because Portuguese immigrants have been there the longest; most immigrants to the mainland see themselves as "transplanted" and remain in close contact with the homeland.

PUERTO RICAN (see also Hispanic)

Individual Authors

534 Cintrón, Humberto. *Frankie Cristo.* New York: Taino, 1972.
A boy escapes poverty by joining the navy and then getting an M.A. in Urban Studies in California. He returns to work with his people in the New York Barrio.

535 Cofer, Julia Ortíz. *The Line of the Sun.* Athens: University of Georgia Press, 1988.
Marisol lives with her family in a tenement in Paterson, New Jersey, and attends a parochial school dominated by Irish and Italian priests and nuns. Her father, an enlistee in the navy, urges her to fit into the American way of life; but her mother is still strongly attached to Puerto Rico and its culture and wants to go back.

536 Cruz, Nicky. *Run, Baby, Run.* Plainfield, NJ: Logos, 1968.
A tough kid is converted to Protestantism and becomes an evangelist who will work in the Barrio.

537 Fernández, Carol. *Sleep of the Innocents.* Houston: Arte Publico, 1990.
Civil unrest in Puerto Rico prompts a rural family to come to New York. The experiences suffered at home and the disruption of values and traditions in the new land take their toll on the family, but the women realize that no matter what happens or where they are, women are restrained by patriarchal society.

538 Mohr, Nicholasa. *El Bronx Remembered.* New York: Harper and Row, 1975. Reprint, Houston: Arte Publico, 1986.
Suitable for young adults. Stories set in the 1940s and 1950s, which deal mainly with the conflicts between new and older

immigrants—such as "Uncle Claudio," in which a man decides that he doesn't want to stay in New York—and between parents and children—such as "A Very Special Pet," in which the youngsters name a hen Joan Crawford and refuse to allow her to be eaten.

539 ———. *In Nueva York*. New York: Dial, 1977. Reprint, Houston: Arte Publico, 1990.

Connected stories about a Puerto Rican community in the Barrio, including that about William, a dwarf, who comes to New York to find his mother, who had deserted him in Puerto Rico forty years earlier. He finds a friend in young Lali, who has recently come to New York through an arranged marriage with a much older man, and together they take night classes in English. In another story Lali runs off with a young new arrival who works in her husband's restaurant.

540 ———. *Nilda*. New York: Harper and Row, 1973. Reprint, Houston: Arte Publico, 1991.

Suitable for young adults. Nilda's mother has come to New York for a better life, but, without knowledge of English or employable skills, she must struggle there to provide for her four children and an eccentric elderly aunt after her husband sickens and cannot work. Nilda grows up in Spanish Harlem in the 1940s, where the Irish priests and nuns and the public school teachers and the police do their best to instill shame in the children for their Puerto Rican culture. The oldest son ends up in jail for selling drugs, but World War II provides the mother with a factory job and another son with enlistment in the navy. Nilda's love of reading and drawing will provide a way for her out of a bleak life after her mother dies.

541 ———. *Rituals of Survival: A Woman's Portfolio*. Houston: Arte Publico, 1985.

Five short stories and a novella about women struggling with poverty and the limitations of female roles in the Puerto Rican communities of New York; one escapes by going to art school.

542 Rivera, Edward. *Family Installments*. New York: Morrow, 1982.

A boy comes from Puerto Rico with his family to the Bronx

and attends the local parochial grade school and then high school, learning meanwhile how to survive on the tough streets, which are patrolled by gangs of boys from other ethnic groups. When his parents return to San Juan, he chooses to attend college in New York. Later he makes the trip back to the island to visit his father and see again his home village, but it will no longer be his own home.

543 Thomas, Piri. *Down These Mean Streets.* New York: Knopf, 1967.

Autobiographical stories about a boy's growing up in Spanish Harlem during the depression. He is the darkest of his four brothers and sisters and therefore the most discriminated against. He has problems at school, is beaten up on the streets, and gets involved in gang wars, drug trafficking, and other crimes, for which he goes to prison.

544 ———. *Saviour, Saviour, Hold My Hand.* New York: Doubleday, 1972.

In this autobiographical novel, a sequel to *Mean Streets,* Piri marries, joins the Pentecostal Church, and works to help young Puerto Ricans; but he comes to be skeptical of the efficacy of Christianity in the Barrio.

545 ———. *Stories from El Barrio.* New York: Knopf, 1978.

For young adults. These stories, some of them humorous, emphasize the importance of family ties and friendship in making a life of poverty bearable and even enjoyable. "Three Mosquiteers" is about tenderfoot boy scouts from the Barrio who get lost in the New Jersey swamps during their first camp outing. "The Konk" tells the story of a sixteen-year-old's getting a painful hair-straightening so that he can look more fashionable. "Coney Island" and "La Peseta" are about a boy's stealing and being punished. "Putting It on for Juanita" tells of a boy who tries to impress a pretty new visitor from Puerto Rico. And "Amigo Brothers" concerns two friends who face each other in a championship boxing match.

546 Vega, Ed. *Mendoza's Dream.* Houston: Arte Publico, 1987.

A collection of interrelated, humorous stories told by a

sympathetic narrator, Mendoza, about Puerto Ricans in the barrio of New York trying to be successful in the U.S.

Anthologies

547 Turner, Faythe. *Puerto Rican Writers at Home in the USA: An Anthology.* Seattle: Open Hand Publishing, 1991.

All the writers here but one, Jesus Colon, were born in or arrived in the U.S. after World War II. Most of the selections are poems, but fiction by the following writers is included: Piri Thomas, Nicholasa Mohr, Rosario Morales, Aurora Levins Morales, and Ed Vega.

Secondary Sources

548 de Laguna, Asela Rodríguez, ed. *Images and Identities: The Puerto Rican in Two World Contexts.* New Brunswick: Transaction, 1987.

The editor's introduction points out that the major theme in this literature is the dualistic nature of the Puerto Rican experience: between the island and the mainland; between barrio and mainstream America; and between two languages and cultures; and that the literature in the United States is influenced by its pluralistic literary traditions. The book contains a section on "Nuyorican" literature, with essays by novelists Piri Thomas and Nicholasa Mohr and by the critics Juan Bruce-Novoa, Nicholas Kanellos, and Charles Tatum. Also includes a survey and critical comment on books written for children.

549 Flores, Juan. "Puerto Rican Literature in the United States." *Redefining American Literary History.* Eds. A. LaVonne Brown Ruoff and Jerry W. Ward, Jr. New York: MLA, 1990.

A historical and critical overview, beginning with works written in Spanish and leading to a discussion of the third or "Nuyorican" stage of English language fiction written in the fifties and sixties, which is characterized by its "combining of autobiographical and imaginative modes of community portrayal" and, like other minority literatures, its "straddling" of two cultures.

550 Mohr, Eugene V. *The Nuyorican Experience: Literature of the Puerto Rican Minority in New York.* Westport, CT: Greenwood, 1982.

A full-length historical and critical survey, beginning with works in Spanish and moving to autobiography in English and then the novel in English, with emphasis on Piri Thomas and Nicholasa Mohr.

ROMANIAN

Individual Authors

551 Neagoe, Peter. *There Is My Heart.* New York: Coward-McCann, 1936.

Peasant John Codreanu hears stories about the abundant opportunities in America from other peasants, as well as more sobering ones from his friend Starevitch; and he decides to take his chances and emigrate. Before he leaves the country, he falls in love with Ileana, another man's wife. When she dies attempting to give birth to his child, he feels that he no longer has any reason to stay in Romania and will go to America, for there his heart is.

552 Vasiliu, Mircea. *Which Way to the Melting Pot?* New York: Doubleday, 1963.

An autobiographical account of a secretary in the Romanian embassy in Washington, D.C., who marries an American woman and becomes an American citizen. With good humor he recounts his struggles to learn English and otherwise adjust to American society.

Secondary Sources

553 Roceric, Alexandra. "Romanian-American Literature." *Ethnic Perspectives in American Literature: Selected Essays on the European Contribution.* Eds. Robert J. Di Pietro and Edward Ifkovic. New York: MLA, 1983.

An introduction to the Romanian contribution to American literature—mostly nonfiction—rather than a historical survey, with a tribute to Neagoe and "an emphasis on Romanian consciousness and memories to highlight the Romanian heritage brought along to the New World."

RUSSIAN (see also Slavic)

Individual Authors

554 Argus, M. K. [Mikhail Konstantinovich Jeleznov]. *Moscow on the Hudson*. New York: Harper and Brothers, 1951.
Autobiographical humorous narratives about a refugee among other Russian émigrés in New York. A popular motion picture with the same title is based on this book.

555 ———. *A Rogue With Ease*. New York: Harper and Brothers, 1953.
A refugee from Soviet Russia, the son of a physician, poses in New York as Prince Basil Saratov, selling fake family heirlooms from a shop on Third Avenue. His friend Andrei Simsky poses as a count. Both realize that Americans are impressed with European royalty and that they can use that awareness to make a living in America.

556 Lebedeff, Vera. *The Heart Returneth*. Philadelphia: Lippincott, 1943.
Aristocratic Russian refugees from the Communist Revolution are living in Detroit and working in auto factories and department stores among the earlier peasant immigrants who had left Russia for economic reasons earlier in the century. Most of the earlier immigrants are financially much more well off than are the aristocrats. Despite this leveling, the aristocrats maintain their titles, hauteur, and social traditions. Andre Borodin, heir to oil wells in the Caucusus, cannot tell his snobbish mother about his secret marriage to the daughter of an ex-peasant, now a wealthy realtor; his sister Anna, hesitates to promote her career as a dress designer; the elder Borodins simply wait, in impoverished gentility, for their possessions and titles to be restored when Communist Russia fails. But the two highest ranking émigrés—Prince Lucian Nemirov, who is earning an engineering degree at night school, and Xenya, a part-time art teacher and daughter of the once most powerful man in Russia, the governor-general of Odessa—shock the colony by determining to return home to work for their native country, regardless of its politics: Germany is about to invade Russia.

557 Nabokov, Vladimir. *Pnin.* Melbourne, Australia: Heinemann, 1960.

The humorous but poignant story of Timofey Pnin, who escapes Russia at the beginning of the Revolution and comes to America by way of London at the start of World War II. In 1945 he gets a position teaching Russian within the German Department at Waindell, a small Eastern college, at which there is little understanding or sympathy between him and his colleagues. After returning from his first vacation—in 1954—to visit friends and fellow émigrés in New England, he decides to stay permanently at Waindell and to buy a house on campus. But he is fired from his position, supposedly for budgetary reasons, and is not sure where to go next.

558 Papashvily, George and Helen Waite. *Anything Can Happen.* New York: Harper and Brothers, 1940.

Autobiographical narratives, some humorous, about a young man who comes to New York with a great spirit of adventure and appreciation. He takes whatever jobs he can get, including, unwittingly, that of a strikebreaker, although, when he discovers what he is doing, he confronts his employers and quits. He moves around the East and Midwest, staying and working with Russian friends, until he marries an American woman and moves with her to a small farm in Virginia.

Secondary Sources

559 Bachman, Carol, and Edward Ifkovic. "Russian-American Literature." *Ethnic Perspectives in American Literature: Selected Essays on the European Contribution.* Eds. Robert J. Di Pietro and Edward Ifkovic. New York: MLA, 1983.

A historical and critical survey. The focus is on works available in English, about half of which are in translation. The largest section of the essay is devoted to Nabokov.

560 Poltoratzky, Nikolai P. "Russian Literature, Literary Scholarship, and Publishing in the United States." *Ethnic Literatures Since 1776: The Many Voices of America.* Eds. Wolodymyr T. Zyla and Wendall Aycock. Lubbock: Proceedings of the Comparative Literature Symposium, Texas Tech University, Jan. 1976. IX (1978): II, 455-501.

A survey of Russian literature in the United States, with comments on all genres, including fiction—but most of it written in Russian. Includes a listing and general comments on a number of writers.

SALVADORAN (see also Hispanic)

Individual Authors

561 Buss, Fran Lapeer. With the assistance of Daisy Cubias. *Journey of the Sparrows*. New York: Dutton, Lodestar Books, 1991.

Suitable for young adults. Most of fifteen-year-old Maria's family has been killed in El Salvador by soldiers, but her mother has gotten the family, including a baby sister, to Mexico, from where Maria, her pregnant sister Julia, and her little brother Oscar are smuggled across the border, in nailed-up crates. They complete the journey to Chicago and are given help by earlier Salvadoran immigrants—both legal and illegal ones—but Maria is sexually harassed at an undercover sweatshop, and her friend is caught and deported by immigration officers. Life becomes a struggle for warmth and food in wintry Chicago, and the local Roman Catholic church tries to work within the law to help them. When Maria learns that her mother and sister are in danger in Mexico, she undertakes the journey to try to save them. Love of family and remembering the symbolic sparrow of her homeland give her the courage she needs.

SCANDINAVIAN (see also Danish, Norwegian, and Swedish)

Secondary Sources

562 Blankner, Frederika. *The History of the Scandinavian Literatures: A Survey of the Literatures of Norway, Sweden, Denmark, Iceland and Finland, from their Origins to the Present Day, including Scandinavian-American Authors and Selected Bibliographies.* New York: Dial, 1938.

The section on American writers is very limited and deals almost exclusively with those who wrote in their native languages rather than in English.

563 Moseley, Ann. "The Land as Metaphor in Two Scandinavian

Immigrant Novels." *MELUS* 5:2 (Summer, 1978), 33-38.
A discussion of the importance of the ownership of land in the trilogies of Rölvaag and Winther.

564 Mossberg, Christer Lennart. *Scandinavian Immigrant Literature.* Boise, ID: Boise State University, Western Writers Series, No. 47, 1981.

A historical survey of the development of Scandinavian-American fiction, both in the Scandinavian languages and in English, mostly about Western and Midwestern farm life, including analyses of the major themes. There are detailed discussions of the trilogies of Rölvaag and Winther.

565 Skårdal, Dorothy Burton. *The Divided Heart: Scandinavian Immigrant Experience Through Literary Sources.* Lincoln: University of Nebraska Press, 1974.

An analysis of the Danish, Norwegian, and Swedish immigrant experience in the United States, including the theme of the assimilation of the second and third generations, through examples from literature, mostly fiction. Most of the works treated are in the original languages, but some attention is given to writers in English. The authors of the excerpts cited are identified only in the notes at the end of the book, so that it is difficult to learn much about an individual novel. Contains a bibliography.

566 ———. "Scandinavian-American Literature." *Ethnic Perspectives in American Literature: Selected Essays on the European Contribution.* Eds. Robert J. Di Pietro and Edward Ifkovic. New York: MLA, 1983.

A historical and critical survey of the literature, mainly fiction, of Danish, Norwegian, and Swedish immigrants and their descendants, in both Scandinavian languages and English, with a discussion of the major themes and critical evaluations of the individual works. Skårdal claims that most fiction written in English by the second generation is not worthwhile and may even be misleading about the Scandinavian immigrant experience. Therefore, she suggests reading the first-rate autobiographies, which she cites, but she does praise the genuine ethnic portraits in the "fictionalized memoirs" of Skulda Banér, Borghild Dahl, Helga Skogsbergh, and Margarethe Erdahl Shank.

SERBIAN (see also Slavic)

Individual Authors

567 Glocar, Emilian. *A Man from the Balkans.* Philadelphia: Dorrance, 1942.

Alexey, who has worked for many years in America, is angered when he learns at his seventieth birthday party that he must register as an alien at the beginning of World War II. He recalls his life in his native village, including the incident that propelled him to America—his killing of his wife and her lover—and his early years in America with a new family. After this recollection, he appreciates what have been his American opportunities and overcomes his anger.

568 Jovanovich, William. *Madmen Must.* New York: Harper and Row, 1978.

John Sirovich is the son of an immigrant father who has worked in the mines in the Midwest and the West and is an official of his community's Serbian lodge, devoted to retaining the heritage and unity of the Serbs, and of an immigrant mother who has worked in factories. John graduates from college in the late 1930s and goes to work as a waiter at a resort in an island off San Diego, where he has many adventures in an attempt to "find himself" as an American. When the war begins, John is reinspired by the heroism of the Serbian immigrants who returned to their country to defend it from the Turks, and he volunteers for Naval Officers School, making a last visit to his parents' ethnic community for his father's approval.

569 Logan, Milla Zenovich. *Bring Along Laughter.* New York: Random House, 1947.

Humorous stories about growing up in an eccentric, but happy and close-knit community of Serbs in San Francisco from the time of the earthquake, during which they all take care of each other and are careful to preserve their old world artifacts and mementos of immigrant heroes. Other stories deal with the retention of old-country, ethnic enemies; the welcoming of new immigrants; and finally to moving out of the old neighborhood into the suburbs and beginning to blend into the American scene.

Secondary Sources

570 Bubresco, Peter D. "American Serbian Literature." *Ethnic Literatures Since 1776: The Many Voices of America*. Eds. Wolodymyr T. Zyla and Wendall Aycock. Lubbock: Proceedings of the Comparative Literature Symposium, Texas Tech University, Jan. 1976. IX (1978): II, 521-45.

   A brief, historical and critical survey of literature by Serbian-Americans, beginning with poetry and moving to fiction. The main themes that Bubresco points out are nostalgia for the homeland and the gradual process of adaptation to the new country.

SLAVIC (see also Croation, Czech, Polish, Russian, Serbian, Slovenian, Slovakian, and Ukrainian)

Secondary Sources

571 Ifkovic, Edward. "Three South Slavic-American Literatures." *Ethnic Perspectives in American Literature: Selected Essays on the European Contribution*. Eds. Robert J. Di Pietro and Edward Ifkovic. New York: MLA, 1983.

   A historical and critical introduction to Slovenian-, Croatian-, and Serbian-American literature of various genres, written in the Slavic languages as well as in English. Mention is made of Joe Magarac, a fictional Croatian steelworker, very much alive in the oral tradition, who came to be a kind of immigrant hero; and there is a summary of and critical comment on Ifkovic's *Anna Marinkovich*. Of novelists, critical attention is paid to the Slovenians Louis Adamic and Frank Mlakar and to the Serbians Emilian Glocar, Milla Zenovich Logan, and William Jovanovich.

Bibliographies

572 Roucek, Joseph S. *American Slavs: A Bibliography*. New York: Bureau of Intercultural Education, 1944.

   Bulgarians, Czechs, Slovaks, Poles, Russians, Ukrainians, and Yugoslavs are included, as are autobiographies, novels, and children's stories, with brief annotations for each.

SLOVAKIAN (see also Slavic)

Individual Authors

573 Bell [Belejcak], Thomas. *Out of This Furnace*. New York: Little, Brown, 1941. Reprint, Pittsburgh: University of Pittsburgh Press, 1976.

A three-generation novel beginning with Djuro "George" Kracha, who comes from his village in Hungarian-ruled Slovakia to work in the steel mills in Braddock, Pennsylvania, in 1881. He buys his own butcher shop, but loses everything in land speculation. His daughter Mary marries Mike Dobrejcak, who is killed in a mill explosion caused by the owners' careless drive for more profits. Their son Dobie, determined that he and his children will not be exploited as his father and grandfather have been, becomes involved in the successful unionization of the steel workers.

574 Novak, Michael. *Naked I Leave*. New York: Macmillan, 1970.

The son of an immigrant steelworker in Pennsylvania who had become a successful foreman before his death by accident in the mill, follows his mother's wishes for him to become a priest. But after some years away from home, and not without guilt, he leaves the priesthood and goes to Europe on an extended trip.

575 Simko, Michael. *Mila Nadaya*. Philadelphia: Dorrance, 1968.

The melodramatic story of the romantic adventures of the most beautiful of the daughters of Gregor and Marta Rodzenik, among the first of the Slovak immigrants to come to Connecticut (1887) and to establish a firm enclave there, complete with its own lodge, church, and thriving business community. Gregor is a butcher/grocer and a leader in the community. Mila ("golden") Nadaya is courted by many men and sees her beauty as a way to climb in American society. Finally, she runs off with Damian Krasny, a suave newcomer to the community and a real estate agent. Too late she learns that he has swindled her family and friends and that he does not plan to set her up in society in New York but to make her a high-class prostitute. She is saved, however, on the highway, by the hometown boy, Ivan Sidorko, a foundry worker and union organizer, who truly loves her and who takes Krasny back to face the music.

Anthologies

576 Cincura, Andrew. *An Anthology of Slovak Literature.* Riverside, CA: University Hardcovers, 1976.

Michael Novak's introductory essay is an overview of Slovak literature and a discussion of the carrying on of its tradition by a few immigrant writers. The collection itself contains mostly works in translation, but there are also excerpts from the novels by Bell and Novak and an unpublished novel by Sonya Jason: *Concomitant Soldier* (1973), the story of an immigrant woman who supports her grandson's unwillingness to serve as a soldier in Vietnam but, at the same time, considers herself a good American who is grateful for its system of courts and trials.

Secondary Sources

577 Laurence, Patricia Ondek. "The Garden in the Mill: The Slovak Immigrant's View of Work." *MELUS* 10:2 (Summer, 1968), 5-17.

Ondek proposes that there is a "sense of vitality and oneness with work and machines" in writings by Slovak-Americans, rather than the image one gets in mainstream literature or histories of immigrant workers.

SLOVENIAN (see also Slavic)

Individual Authors

578 Adamic, Louis. *Grandsons.* New York: Harper and Brothers, 1935.

In the U.S. Army during World War I, the narrator, a Slovenian immigrant, meets Peter Gale, whose grandfather had immigrated from a village near his own home. Over several years they keep in touch, as Peter tells the story of his family: his grandfather had been killed in the Haymarket riots; his father had worked in Pennsylvania steel mills, but has risen to the middle class; his brother Andy becomes a high power in the Los Angeles branch of a national crime syndicate; his cousin Jack is a heroic union organizer; and his sister marries into high society. Hearing the stories of these great differences in the lives of members of one family, the narrator is affected, but he himself cannot find his own identity, and he continues to drift from place to place.

579 Mlakar, Frank. *He, the Father*. New York: Harper and Brothers, 1950.

Osip Princevich assaults his father and steals from him the money which he and his sweetheart Lenka need for passage to America. In Cuyahoga City, Ohio, he works at a wire mill, and they find a sense of community with other Slovenes through their social center, Smrekar's Saloon. But Osip cannot overcome the guilt he feels for his behavior to his father, and after losing a son, undergoing conflicts with a second son, and Lenka's imprisonment for bootlegging, Osip returns to his Slovenian village to make an atonement.

Anthologies

580 Gobetz, Giles Edward and Adele Donchenko, eds. *Anthology of Slovenian-American Literature*. Willoughby Hills, Ohio: Slovenian Research Center of America, 1977.

Contains fiction, in addition to memoirs and essays, either originally written in or translated into English, by twenty-three writers, three of them Canadian. The collection is divided into four sections: "Bridges," pieces with old and new country elements and connections; "Give Us This Day," pieces about work; "All Kinds of People," pieces which underscore the diversity and individuality of immigrants; and "A Soul Divided," pieces which illustrate immigrants torn between two worlds. Part Five gives background information on Slovenia, leading to an overview of Slovenian-American literature. Fictional pieces are Daniela Dolenc's "Survivors"; Louis Adamic's "The Old Alien by the Kitchen Window," an account of the life of a worker in a wire factory in Cleveland; "Osip Buys a Home in Chicken Village," an excerpt from Frank Mlakar's *He, The Father*; Stanley Zupan, "The Cross-Spider," about an immigrant's childhood in Slovenia; and John Modic, "Being Naked Is a Sin," about an immigrant woman's disapproval of her nephew's going about in "underwear" to play basketball.

Secondary Sources

581 Gobetz, Giles Edward. "Slovenian-American Literature." *Ethnic Literatures Since 1776: The Many Voices of America*. Eds. Wolodymyr T. Zyla and Wendall Aycock. Proceedings of the

Comparative Literature Symposium, Texas Tech University, Jan. 1976. IX (1978): I, 547-68.

A historical and critical survey of works, starting in the 1680s with travel reports or missionaries' journals written in Slovenian. The two best-known fiction writers, Adamic and Mlakar, are described at the end.

582 Prosen, Rose Mary. "Slovenian-American Literature: Louis Adamic's *Grandsons* and Frank Mlakar's *He, the Father*." *MELUS* 5:4 (Winter 1978), 52-62.

Contends that Adamic's novel deals with the question of what it takes to be an American, but Mlakar's, the better book, deals with what it takes to be a man.

SPANISH

Individual Authors

583 De Pereda, Prudencio. *Windmills in Brooklyn*. New York: Atheneum, 1960.

A boy's recollections of his growing up in a Spanish community in Brooklyn. The boy wants to be a writer, learns Spanish, and is interested in the land of his heritage. Therefore, he tells of the lives of his special heroes: his grandfather and grandfather's friend Agapito—both *teverionos*, tricksters in the cigar business, often making their profits off wealthy priests. He also tells tales of his grandmother and a kindly older woman who has initiated him into sex—their childhoods in Spain, their transference to the U.S., and their adjustments there. He also describes the daily life of the community: their celebrations and dance shows and their meetings at *La Espan*, the local social club.

SWEDISH (see also Scandinavian)

Individual Authors

584 Banér, Skulda. *Latchstring Out*. New York: Houghton Mifflin, 1944.

Stories of a girl, the daughter of immigrants, growing up in a mining community in the Upper Peninsula of Michigan in the early twentieth century. Though they are a minority in the community, the Swedes have their own Lutheran church and maintain their holiday celebrations and other traditions. The children are bilingual and are teased by other children as foreigners.

585 Budd, Lillian. *Land of Strangers*. Philadelphia: Lippincott, 1944.

Carl Peterson leaves his homeland to avoid military conscription as well as to make his fortune, as a friend, writing home from Chicago, has insisted he can do. He works on a passenger liner to earn his own passage money and eventually immigrates through Castle Garden, working in New York until he can get to Chicago. Eventually Ellen comes to join him, and they are able to marry, as they had not been allowed to in Sweden. But they must struggle to make a living, particularly through the depression years. Years later, Carl returns to see his hometown again.

586 Cannon, Cornelia James. *Red Rust*. Boston: Little, Brown, 1928.

Immigrant Matt Swenson goes to Minnesota to develop and grow a rust-resistant wheat grain. He and his family endure many hardships until they are successful.

587 Cather, Willa. *O Pioneers!* Boston: Houghton Mifflin, 1913.

After her immigrant father dies, Alexandra Bergson takes over the family farm in Nebraska. She is so effective in using new agricultural techniques that she can lend money to pay the passage money for other immigrants and educate her brother at the state university. After many years, she marries her long-time sweetheart, Carl Lindstrum, who had left the area to learn the engravers trade.

588 Engstrand, Stuart David. *They Sought for Paradise*. New York: Harper and Brothers, 1939.

Nils Nilsson's betrothed, Helga, has come under the power of Eric Jansson, a charismatic evangelist, whose followers have given him money to build a New Jerusalem in Illinois. Nils follows the band overland by ski to Norway, by ship to America, and then by boat and oxcart to their "promised land." Even after several years of working for Jansson, Nils is not permitted to marry Helga, and he leaves the colony to farm his own land and marry the American Mary Reilly. After she dies of cholera and

Jansson is finally exposed as a fraud, Helga becomes Nils' wife.

589   Havighurst, Walter. *Winds of Spring*. New York: Macmillan, 1940.
      Among the pioneers in Wisconsin in the 1840s through the 1860s is an immigrant scholar, Jan, who lives in a log cabin in the woods and becomes a recognized ornithologist.

590   Moberg, Vilhelm. *The Emigrants*. Translated by Gustav Lannestock. New York: Simon and Schuster, 1951. Reprint, New York: Popular Library.
      The first of a trilogy. Karl Oskar Nilsson, his wife, young son and younger brother leave Sweden in the 1840s to immigrate to the U.S., because they have nearly starved on their small farm. The ocean voyage is long and difficult, but they arrive safely in New York in the summer of 1850.

591   ———. *Time on Earth*. Translated by Gustav Lannestock. New York: Simon and Schuster, 1965.
      The conclusion of the trilogy. The family homestead in Minnesota, dealing with agricultural problems and attacks from Indians. Karl's younger brother leaves to dig gold in the West, but returns after having been unsuccessful and nearly dying.

592   ———. *Unto a Good Land*. Translated by Gustav Lannestock. New York: Simon and Schuster, 1954.
      The second of the trilogy. The Nilssons travel overland from New York to Minnesota, where they find land in the wilderness to homestead.

593   Pawle, Katherine [Mrs. Dermoth Darby]. *Mural for a Later Day*. New York: Dodd, Mead, 1938.
      A story of the founding of New Sweden on the Delaware River. Johan Prinz, the four-hundred-pound leader of the community, is an ambitious trader.

594   Schlytter, Leslie Evan. *Tall Brothers*. New York: Appleton-Century, 1941.
      A Swedish farm couple in a Wisconsin lumbertown between 1900 and 1925 are in conflict with two unscrupulous lumbermen.

595 Skogsbergh, Helga. *Comes the Day, Comes a Way*. Chicago: Covenant, 1960.

In this first part of a trilogy, two young couples, the Isaksons and the Hansons, recent immigrants living in Duluth at the end of the nineteenth century, go to the Wisconsin shores of Lake Superior to homestead. In cabins near each other in the wilderness, Betty and Emma deliver each other's babies and adapt to a rustic life, as the families see more and more settlers arriving and the nearest town growing to include shops and churches. Mr. Hanson conducts devotional services because they have no pastor of their own, and the Swedish families celebrate Christmas together in their own style.

596 ———. *From These Shores*. Chicago: Covenant, 1963.

The second part of the trilogy covers the next ten years, during which time more children have been born, more settlers have arrived, and the town has grown to include more stores and churches, a post office, a saw mill and a consolidated school. Emma Hanson's sister has recently come from Sweden and is employed as a maid in Duluth but will come to attend Emma at the birth of her next child. Papa Hanson gets a job delivering mail to the Finnish community upshore, and Ingrid Hanson leaves for college in Duluth to be a teacher.

597 ———. *From These Shores*. Chicago: Covenant, 1975.

An abridged version of the trilogy in one volume.

598 ———. *That Was Then*. Chicago: Covenant, 1969.

Ingrid Hanson, at seventy, returns in the 1960s to visit the settlement where she grew up, recollecting her childhood among the hardy homesteaders and noting the changes that have occurred in the interceding fifty years.

SYRIAN AND LEBANESE

Individual Authors

599 Geha, Joseph. *Through and Through: Toledo Stories*. St. Paul, MN: Greywolf, 1990.

Stories of Syrian and Lebanese immigrant families in Toledo, Ohio, from the 1930s to the 1980s, with a focus on generational conflicts—e.g., "Everything, Everything," in which Mama does not want Barbara to have her own apartment—or conflicts between new and older immigrants or those from other ethnic groups—e.g., "News from Phoenix," in which Sofia avoids and rejects the Jewish couple who are her husband's friends and advisors.

600 Rihani, Ameen. *The Book of Khalid.* 1911. Abridged, Beirut: Albert Rihani, 1973.

Two young men sail for America and jump overboard at Ellis Island, swimming to shore, rather than undergo the medical examination for trachoma. In New York, they peddle the religious icons and trinkets they have brought from the Holy Land. One of them, bored with American life and missing his own country, sails back with a goodly amount of money.

601 Rizk, Salom. *Syrian Yankee.* Garden City, NY: Doubleday, Doran, 1943.

An autobiographical novel about a boy growing up in abject poverty in Syria, with his grandmother, who has concealed the fact that he has an American father. Eventually, Salom is able to go to Iowa to join his American family. As Sam, he works, ineptly, at a meatpacking plant in Sioux City, and then as a traveling salesman, before he determines that he wants to be educated. He studies in the public school with children and does so well that he becomes a public speaker, much in demand for his praises of America. He scolds American students for not fully appreciating their free educational opportunities and the general freedoms in their lives.

UKRAINIAN (see also Slavic)

Individual Authors

602 Block, Maria Halun. *Marya of Clark Avenue.* New York: Coward-McCann, 1957.

For young adults. Marya Palenko grows up in Cleveland in the 1920s. Her family moves out of their ethnic enclave when her father opens an upholstery shop on Clark Avenue. Marya feels like an alien, particularly for being out of synch with other Christians in her family's celebration of Easter and Christmas according to the Eastern Orthodox calendar and rites. But after her school friends and her teacher come to her family's Christmas celebration and enjoy themselves, she stops feeling ashamed of her heritage and believes that she can be both Ukrainian and American without conflict.

Secondary Sources

603 Shtohyrn, Dmytro M. "Ukrainian Literature in the United States: Trends, Influences, Achievements." *Ethnic Literatures Since 1776: The Many Voices of America*. Eds. Wolodymyr T. Zyla and Wendall Aycock. Proceedings of the Comparative Literature Symposium, Texas Tech University, Jan. 1976. IX (1978) II, 569-590.

   Begins with a brief historical-social background of immigrant life and the beginning of cultural activities in the U.S.; moves to a discussion of post-World War II immigrants and to the second generation, who focussed on political activities in the Ukraine or who were mostly poets. Discusses Block's contribution to children's literature in her presentations of Ukrainian immigrant life.

VIETNAMESE (see also Asian)

Individual Authors

604 Butler, Robert Olen. *A Good Scent from a Strange Mountain.* New York: Henry Holt, 1992.

   Winner of the Pulitzer Prize for fiction. A collection of stories about Vietnamese refugees in and around New Orleans, particularly Versailles and Lake Charles on the Gulf. The characters reminisce about their childhoods in Vietnam, the war, their escapes, their immigration, and their learning to become American. About half are told by women, and most stories are told in the first person. Some themes include finding old friends and renewing friendships, the carrying on of political battles, the accommodation of Christianity and Buddhism, and the rapid assimilation of American-born children.

605 Garland, Sherry. *Shadow of the Dragon.* New York: Harcourt Brace Jovanovich, 1993.

For young adults. Sixteen-year-old Danny, a refugee, fits in with his American friends in Houston, although his home life is traditional. Cousin Song Le comes to live with them after having spent five years in a Communist re-education camp. Song Le joins a Vietnamese gang, which fights against an American Skinhead gang.

606 Hayslip, Le Ly. *Child of War, Woman of Peace*. New York: Doubleday, 1993.

A sequel to *Heaven and Earth*, and a chronological, autobiographical narrative, it is included here because it fills in the gaps in the earlier book. It tells of the narrator's difficult adjustment to life in California after she is widowed twice and must support her three sons by working as a domestic, then in a factory and restaurant, until, with financial stability, she becomes a social activist and founds the East Meets West Foundation, a relief organization to help the needy in Vietnam.

607 ———. *When Heaven and Earth Changed Places*. New York: Doubleday, 1989.

Though an autobiography, it is structured like a novel. Le Ly, more than ten years after having left Vietnam in the middle of the war, as the wife of an American businessman, returns to visit her family. Interspersed with her impressions of the changes in her homeland and her family are the recollections of her childhood and youth: fighting for and then fleeing from the Viet Cong, peddling on the black market, and surviving the upheaval caused by the war and by the concentration of American troops in Saigon. As an American citizen, she is grateful for the opportunities afforded her sons, but she misses her culture, her family, and her native land.

608 Tran Van Dinh. *Blue Dragon, White Tiger: A Tet Story*. Philadelphia: TriAm Press, 1983.

Tran Van Minh escapes the Communists by boat with twenty other intellectuals. They are robbed and raped by Thai bandits before finding refuge in Thailand, where they are helped to go to the United States.

609 Wartski, Maureen Crane. *A Boat to Nowhere*. Philadelphia: Westminster, 1980. Reprint, New York: Signet, 1981.

For young adults. Kien, a fourteen-year-old orphan comes to a small, isolated village in Vietnam and persuades Mai, her little brother, and her grandfather to escape aboard a fishing boat. They sail for many days, undergoing fear of pirates, storms, sickness, and starvation, before they are picked up by an American freighter.

610 ———. *A Long Way from Home*. Philadelphia: Westminster, 1980. Reprint, New York: Signet, 1981.

For young adults. The sequel to *A Boat from Nowhere*. Kien, now fifteen, is sponsored by the Olsons, who live in California. He hates school because he is called names and pushed around by the other boys. He runs away to a seaside town where, he has heard, there is a Vietnamese colony. He gets in trouble by being involved with the fishing disputes between his new friends and the long-time Americans, and he returns to his adoptive parents.

WEST INDIAN

Individual Authors

611 Fox, Paula. *A Servant's Tale*. San Francisco: North Point, 1984. Reprint, New York: Penguin, 1986.

Luisa de la Cueva, the daughter of a plantation owner's son and a servant girl, lives in the servant's quarters of a large hacienda on a small Caribbean island. When a revolution begins, her family flee to New York, where they live in a barrio tenement. She works as a maid in Long Island, marries, and has a son. Though an American citizen, she cherishes, for many years, the idea of returning to her home, where she believes she may inherit the old property. When she does return, she finds that the sugar plantation now contains a plastic factory and much cheap housing and that her old enemies now run the village. She returns to the U.S.

612 Kincaid, Jamaica. *Lucy*. New York: Farrar, Strauss, and Giroux, 1990.

A young woman leaves her home in the West Indies to be a nanny in New York, completely cutting her ties to her family by refusing to respond to letters or to visit them. Nor can she respond to the kindness of her employers, for she resents the discrepancies between the lives of rich and poor, black and white. After a year or so, preferring independence to security, she leaves them to take her own apartment and her chances with another kind of job in New York.

613   Lamming, George. *In the Castle of My Skin*. New York: McGraw-Hill, 1953.

An autobiographical novel in which young Lamming and his friends grow up in rural Barbados, in a close community of church and family. When the social and political unrest in Trinidad spreads to Barbados, Lamming goes to America, and there he becomes aware of the plight of other Caribbean immigrants, who have lost a sense of their racial heritage.

614   Marshall, Paule. *Brown Girl, Brown Stones*. New York: Random House, 1959. Reprint, New York: Avon, 1970.

Silla Boyce comes to Brooklyn in the 1920s for a better life: through hard work and economy, she hopes to acquire her own property in a better neighborhood and respectability within the West Indian immigrant community. However, her husband Deighton, a fancy man and womanizer, wants to return to Barbados with their money and live in style there. When Silla learns that Deighton has inherited land in Barbados, she sells it; but he retrieves the money, spends it on foolish, expensive gifts for his daughters, and leaves home to join a fanatic religious society. Their daughter Selina is torn in her loyalty, but after World War II, during which time Silla's war plant job has enabled Selina to go to college, she rejects the Barbadian Association as provincial and elitist, an imitation of white society, and goes to Barbados to learn about her heritage on her own.

615   ———. *Praisesong for the Widow*. New York: Putnam's, 1983.

Avey Johnson recalls her life in Brooklyn before 1945: mainly the poverty of it, but also the dances and parties in the West Indian community. She decides to sell her home in White Plains, New York, and return to Barbados to live more fully within her African traditions and to teach them to her grandson.

616   ———. *Reena and Other Stories*. Old Westbury, NY: Feminist Press, 1983.

Stories focussing on women: in "To Da-duh In Memorium," a

woman recalls being taken as a child to visit her grandmother in Barbados and experiencing with her a kind of debate on whether life on the island or in Brooklyn is better. The child seems to have won the argument, but the grown woman realizes that she was wrong. The collection also contains an introductory essay on the oral tradition of the immigrant generation, from which Marshall learned to be a writer.

617 McKay, Claude. *Home to Harlem.* New York: Harper and Brothers, 1928. Reprint, New York: Pocket Books, 1963.
    Ray is born in Haiti, son of a formerly prominent official in the government, and a man who has known a stable home life—both as a son and a husband. He comes to Howard University in the 1920s to study, but must quit and takes a job as a railroad porter. He meets Jake, a rootless American Black, who leads a transient life and is in search of a good time in the Harlem jazz clubs. Each affects the other: Ray rejects the white values of colonial Haiti, and Jake decides to move to Chicago, settle down with his fiancée, and raise a family.

Secondary Sources

618 Rahming, Melvin B. *The Evolution of the West Indian's Image in the Afro-American Novel.* Millwood, NY: Associated Faculty, 1986.
    The focus is on the Afro-American novel and on how American Black writers have influenced West Indian writers to emphasize their Negro heritage rather than white values. Chapter Four treats West Indian novelists Lamming, Marshall, and McKay.

YUGOSLAVIAN (see Croatian, Serbian, and Slovenian)

THE GENERAL IMMIGRANT EXPERIENCE

Anthologies

619 Blicksilver, Edith, ed. *The Ethnic American Woman: Problems, Protests, Lifestyles.* Dubuque, IA: Kendall/Hunt, 1978, 1981.
    A collection of various genres, written by women, representing twenty ethnic groups. Fiction about the immigrant

experience includes that by Chinese, Edith Eaton and Maxine Hong Kingston; Japanese, Hisaye Yamamoto; Puerto Rican, Nicholasa Mohr; Jewish, Grace Paley; and Polish, Monica Krawczyk.

620 Brown, Wesley and Amy Ling, eds. *Imagining America: Stories from the Promised Land.* New York: Persea Books, 1991.

A collection of thirty-seven stories divided into four content groups: Arriving, Belonging, Crossings, and Remembering. Asians, Hispanics, West Indians, and European immigrant groups are all represented, as well as are Native and African-Americans.

621 Butcher, Philip, ed. *The Ethnic Image in Modern American Literature, 1900-1950*, Vol. 1. Washington, D.C.: Howard University Press, 1984. 2 vols.

Of interest are the following sections, which contain fiction about the immigrant experience: 1. "Discovering America: The Promised Land"; 2. "Americanization: Into the Main Stream"; and 6. "The Ghetto: Haven and Hell." The fiction is exclusively about the European experience.

622 Faderman, Lillian and Barbara Bradshaw, eds. *Speaking for Ourselves.* 2nd ed. Glenview, IL: Scott Foresman, 1975.

A textbook for high-school or college students, with introductory essays, about ethnic groups that have had "distinct problems of adjustment to American life," and therefore includes selections from Native American as well as black writers. Changes from the first edition include the terms "Asian" for "Oriental"; "Chicano" for "Mexican-Americans"; and "white ethnic" for Europeans. Representing the Asian groups are Japanese, "The Widower" by Ferris Takahashi; "The Legend of Miss Sasagawara" by Hisaye Yamamoto; and "The Eggs of the World" and "The Seventh Street Philosopher" by Toshio Mori; Chinese, an excerpt from *Chinatown Family* by Lin Yutang; and Filipino, "The Day the Dancers Came" by Bienvenido Santos. Hispanic stories are Puerto Rican, Piri Thomas, "Alien Turf" from *Down These Mean Streets*; Mexican, Américo Paredes, "The Legend of Gregorio Cortez"; and Oscar Zeta Acosta, "Perla Is a Pig." Jewish stories are Bernard Malamud, "The First Seven Years"; Philip Roth, "Eli the Fanatic"; and Grace Paley, "The Long Distance Runner." And "white ethnic" stories are Spanish,

Prudencio de Pereda, "Conquistador"; Italian, Pietro Di Donato, from *Christ in Concrete*; Greek, Harry Petrakis, "The Wooing of Ariadne;" Polish, Richard Bankowsky, from *After Pentecost*; Irish, James T. Farrell, "The Oratory Contest"; and Basque, Robert Laxalt, from *Sweet Promised Land.*

623 Fisher, Dexter, ed. *The Third Woman: Minority Women Writers of the United States.* Boston: Houghton Mifflin, 1980.

The sections on Asian and Hispanic women contain fiction on the immigrant experience by Mexican, Estela Portillo; Chinese, Maxine Hong Kingston; and Japanese, Hisaye Yamamoto, Karen Tei Yamashita, and Wakako Yamauchi. Also contains bibliographies for each group.

624 Gallo, Donald R., ed. *Join In: Multi-Ethnic Short Stories by Outstanding Authors for Young Adults.* New York: Delacorte, 1993.

Stories about Cambodians, Cubans, Chinese, Laotians, Japanese, Puerto Ricans, and Vietnamese in the U.S.

625 Handlin, Oscar, ed. *Children of the Uprooted.* New York: Braziller, 1966.

The collection is divided into three historical periods, with a background essay for each, and includes selections of fiction about the immigrant experience by second-generation writers: Norwegian, Anthony Rud; Armenian, Harry Barba and William Saroyan; Italian, Jerre Mangione and John Fante; Dutch, Peter De Vries; Polish, Richard Bankowsky; and Jewish, Delmore Schwartz and Isaac Rosenfeld.

626 Ifkovic, Edward, ed. *American Letter: Immigrant and Ethnic Writing.* Englewood Cliffs, NJ: Prentice Hall, 1975.

Selections from various genres, including fiction, and many ethnic groups, with a general historical introduction and separate introductions to the five sections: "What Is America? Who Is an American?"; "The Old Country"; "Reborn in the Promised Land"; "American Children: Alienation and Assimilation"; and "The Future: Cultural Pluralism or Melting Pot or What?"

627 Miller, Wayne Charles, ed. *A Gathering of Ghetto Writers: Irish,*

Italian, Jewish, Black, and Puerto Rican. New York: New York University Press, 1972.

The purpose of this collection, as explained in the lengthy introduction, is to illustrate the commonality of the experiences of ghetto people, so that there may be a more enlightened awareness about ethnic groups both within and without the ghetto, who may be "separated by ignorance and suspicion and bigotry." Stories about Irish immigrants by J. W. Sullivan and James T. Farrell; about Italian immigrants by Pietro Di Donato, John Fante, and Michael De Capite; about Jewish immigrants by Michael Gold, Anzia Yezierska, and Henry Roth; and about Puerto Ricans by Piri Thomas.

628   Mirikitani, Janice, ed. *Third World Women.* San Francisco: Third World Communications, 1972.

Selections of poetry, essays, and fiction by black, Asian, and Hispanic writers.

629   Newman, Katharine D., ed. *The American Equation: Literature in a Multi-ethnic Culture.* Boston: Allyn and Bacon, 1971.

A collection of poetry, essays, and fiction in four sections by the founder of *MELUS*, which includes many ethnic groups. In the introduction, Newman emphasizes that the U.S. is made up of "minorities." each contributing to the color of the country. Pertinent stories follow. Section 1, "Self-Definition," in which one's own people are described: Filipino, José Garcia Villa, "Untitled Story"; Japanese, Yamamoto, "Seventeen Syllables"; Greek, Petrakis, "Journal of a Wife Beater"; Jewish, Sholom Aleichem, "Mottel in America." Section 3, "The Complementary Self," which explores the love-hate relationships of one's group: Jewish, Bernard Malamud, "Angel Levine." Section 4, "The American Metaphor": German, Theodore Dreiser, "Old Rogram and His Theresa"; and Armenian, William Saroyan, "Seventy Thousand Assyrians."

630   ———. *Ethnic American Short Stories.* New York: Washington Square Press, 1975.

A collection of stories chosen to illustrate the themes of conflict between individual and family, between generations, and in growing up in a society which offers both social limitations and great opportunities for "mental and emotional growth and spiritual expansion." Stories about the immigrant experience are Jewish, Hugh Nissenson, "The Law"; Greek, Spiro Athanas, "A Bag of Oranges"; Irish, Philip F. O'Connor, "The Gift Bearer"; Irish-Cuban, Richard Farina, "Long Time Coming and a Long Time Gone"; Italian, Jordan Pecile, "A Piece of Polenta"; Norwegian, Eric Larsen, "Feast"; and Hawaiian-Japanese, Alan and Take Beekman, "No Place Beneath the Rising Sun"; Polish, John Zebrowski, "Job Hunt"; Mexican, Fray Angelico Chávez, "The Colonel and the Santo"; Chinese, Frank Chin, "Yes, Daddy"; and Cuban, José Yglesias, "The Gun in the Closet."

631 Ravitz, Abe C., ed. *The American Disinherited: A Profile in Fiction.* Belmont, CA: Dickenson, 1970.

Stories about the American down-and-out; those about the immigrant experience are Jewish, Bruno Lessing, "The End of the Task," Ben Hecht, "The Sybarite," Saul Bellow, "Two Morning Monologues," Bernard Malamud, "The Mourners"; Italian, John Fante, "Odyssey of a Wop"; Irish, James T. Farrell, "The Benefits of American Life"; and Puerto Rican, John Figueroa, "Antonio and the Great World."

632 Reed, Ishmael, Katherine Trueblood, and Shawn Wong. *The Before Columbus Foundation Fiction Anthology: Selections from the American Book Awards, 1980-1990.* New York: W.W. Norton.

Reed's introductory essay redefines the "mainstream" of American literature as a much more inclusive "ocean." The thirty stories represent Asian, Hispanic West Indian, and European immigrant groups, as well as Native and African-Americans.

633 Rico, Barbara Roche and Sandra Mano, eds. *American Mosaic: Multicultural Readings in Context.* Boston: Houghton Mifflin, 1991.

Designed for college classroom use, this anthology contains selections from various genres, in nine sections, arranged chronologically and by ethnic group, with historical introductions to each section. Fiction on the immigrant experience includes excerpts from the novels or short story collections of Norwegian, Ole Rølvaag; Irish, Myra Kelly; Jewish, Anzia Yezierska and Cynthia Ozick; Chinese, Sui Sin Far and Maxine Hong Kingston; Puerto Rican, Piri Thomas, Nicholasa Mohr, and Judith Ortiz

Cofer; Japanese, Toshio Mori, John Okada, and Hisaye Yamamoto; Mexican, José Villareal, Arturo Islas, and Sandra Cisneros; and Vietnamese, Tran Van Dinh.

634 Seller, Maxine Schwartz., ed. *Immigrant Women*. Philadelphia: Temple University Press, 1981.

A collection of essays, historical pieces, memoirs, autobiographical sketches, and fiction by and about women immigrants. The collection is divided into eight thematic sections: "Reasons for Coming," "Surviving in a New Land," "Work," "Family," "Community Life," "Education," "Social Activists," and "Daughters and Granddaughters." Relevant fiction is by Irish, Mary Doyle Curran; Chinese, Maxine Hong Kingston; Jewish, Anzia Yezierska; Polish, Monica Krawczyk; Norwegian, Ole Rölvaag; and West Indian, Paule Marshall. There is a bibliographical essay at the end.

635 Shaw, Harry and Ruth Davis, eds. *Americans One and All*. New York: Harper and Brothers, 1947.

A collection of twenty-three stories, each about a different ethnic or immigrant group. Writers of stories about the immigrant experience are the following: Norwegian, Kathryn Forbes; Italian, Guido D'Agostino; Russian, George Papashvily; Dutch, David De Jong; Serbian, Milla Logan; Armenian, William Saroyan; Slovenian, Frank Mlakar; and German, Ruth Suckow.

636 Simon, Myron, ed. *Ethnic Writers in America*. New York: Harcourt Brace Jovanovich, 1972.

A collection of stories, poetry, and essays. Stories about the Jewish experience are by Abraham Cahan, Leo Rosten, Michael Gold, Albert Halper, Saul Bellow, and Bernard Malamud; stories about the Armenian experience are by William Saroyan, Leon Surmelian, and Richard Hagopian; and a story about the Irish experience is by James T. Farrell.

637 Walker, Scott. *Stories from the American Mosaic*. St. Paul, MN: Graywolf, 1990.

Among others, stories about immigrant life are the following: Syrian, Joseph Geha, "Monkey Business"; West Indian, Jamaica Kincaid, "Mariah"; Indian, Bharati Mukherjee, "The Tenant"; Iranian, Nahid Rachlin, "Journey of Love"; Chinese, Amy Tan,

"Two Kinds"; Japanese, Yoshiko Uchida, "Tears of Autumn"; Japanese-Portuguese-Hawaiian, Susan Nunes, "A Moving Day"; and Mexican, Mary Helen Ponce, "Enero".

Secondary Sources

638 Avery, Evalyn Gross. "In Limbo: Immigrant Children and the American Dream." *MELUS* 8:4 (Winter, 1981), 25-31.

Through a discussion of two Jewish novels (Yezierska's *Bread Givers* and Michael Gold's *Jews Without Money*) and two Italian novels (Di Donato's *Christ in Concrete* and Puzo's *Fortunate Pilgrim*), Avery proposes that, whereas male children are disenchanted with the United States, female children feel fortunate to be there.

639 Baker, Houston A., Jr., ed. *Three American Literatures: Essays on Chicano, Native American, and Asian-American Literature for Teachers of American Literature.* New York: MLA, 1982.

Relevant essays are Luis Leal and Pepe Barron, "Chicano Literature: An Overview"; Raymond A. Paredes, "The Evolution of Chicano Literature"; Jeffrey Paul Chan, Frank Chin, Lawson Fusao Inada, and Shawn H. Wong, "An Introduction to Chinese-American and Japanese-American Literatures"; and Lawson Fusao Inada, "Of Place and Displacement: The Range of Japanese-American Literature."

640 Blake, Fay M. *The Strike in the American Novel.* Metuchen, N.J.: Scarecrow Press, 1972.

Begins with a discussion of anti-immigrant novels in which immigrants are characterized as barbarians and troublemakers, and leads to the more favorable presentations of immigrant workers by Sinclair Lewis, Upton Sinclair, Jack Conroy, and John Dos Passos, and by immigrant writers Thomas Bell, Samuel Ornitz, and Abraham Cahan.

641 Boelhower, William Q. "The Ethnic Trilogy: A Poetics of Cultural Passage." *MELUS* 12:4 (Winter, 1985), 7-23.

Suggests that most writers of trilogies, especially between 1900 and 1940, were immigrant and ethnic and that the trilogy served as an experimental way of integrating American culture and becoming American. In that context, discusses Rölvaag, Winther, Farrell, Di Donato and others.

642 ————. *Through a Glass Darkly: Ethnic Semiosis in American Literature*. New York: Oxford University Press, 1987.

Challenges the idea that mainstream and ethnic literatures are or can be separated. Contends that ethnic literature is American literature. In this light, he examines selected fiction, including that about the immigrant experience.

643 Chametzky, Jules. "Some Notes on Immigration, Ethnicity, Acculturation." *MELUS* 11:1 (Spring, 1984), 45-51.

Argues that, in the fiction of immigrants and their descendants, similar issues are developed: "the common ground deals with the response to the thwarting and frustration of the promise and potential of American life and its cultural elements."

644 Di Pietro, Robert J. and Edward Ifkovic, eds. *Ethnic Perspectives in American Literature: Selected Essays on the European Contribution*. New York: MLA, 1983.

Twelve critical and historical essays which provide an overview of the literature, each written by a member of the group in question. The essays are listed separately in this bibliography. The editors' introduction briefly outlines the history of immigration in the United States and notes that definitions of "ethnic literature" may vary, but that all of it has in common certain features: it is "shaped in some way by the writers' contact with the dominant society" and often "display[s] generational differences." The editors also summarize the specific themes as pointed out by the various ethnic groups.

645 Dryud, David L. "Varieties of Marginality: The Treatment of the European Immigrant in the Midwestern Frontier Novel." Ph.D. dissertation, Purdue University, 1979.

Deals with novels published between 1880 and 1970 and discusses four major themes which they illustrate: family tensions, cultural deprivation, Yankee resentment, and nature as an obstacle.

646 *Ethnic Women Writers I. MELUS* 7:3 (Fall, 1980).

Contains essays about Jewish, Anzia Yezierska; Polish,

Monica Krawczyk; and Japanese, Hisaye Yamamoto.

647 Fairbanks, Carol. *Prairie Women: Images in American and Canadian Fiction.* New Haven, CT: Yale University Press, 1986.

Poses the view as corrective that prairie women in fiction are more often shown as heroes, not victims, particularly in the novels that deal with immigrant women.

648 Fairbanks, Carol and Sara Brooks Sundberg. *Farm Women on the Prairie Frontier: A Sourcebook for Canada and the United States.* Metuchen, NJ: Scarecrow Press, 1983.

Contains background on the settling of the prairies, the contributions of women to that settling, and an essay about women in relevant fiction. About half of the book is an annotated bibliography of relevant fiction, some of it about immigrants.

649 Ferraro, Thomas J. *Ethnic Passages: Literary Immigrants in Twentieth-Century America.* Chicago: University of Chicago Press, 1993.

The introduction explains that immigrant literature has been "undervalued and misread," and goes on to explain why it should not be. Five critical essays follow: on Puzo, *The Godfather* narratives; Yezierska, *Breadgivers*; Roth, *Call It Sleep*; Henry Miller's autobiographical writings; and Maxine Hong Kingston, *The Woman Warrior*. The conclusion points to the desire that new and forthcoming immigrant literature will also be taken seriously as valid contributions to American literature.

650 Gartner, Carol Blicker. "A New Mirror for America: The Fiction of the Immigrant of the Ghetto, 1890-1930." Ph.D. dissertation, New York University, 1970.

Argues that immigrant fiction played a significant role in American literature, in that it introduced new sources of material and revitalized the current fiction. The novels are seen to be concerned mainly with the themes of the immediate problems of living in the new world, of deciding how much of one's culture to give up in adjusting, of alienation and poor living conditions, and of balancing freedom and opportunities for advancement with the obstacles in their way. Those treated most fully are the Jews Cahan, Yezierska, and Montague Glass, and the Irish Myra Kelly; briefer discussions are on the Jewish writers John Cournos,

Ludwig Lewisohn, Elias Tobenkin, Herman Bernstein, Hyman and Lester Cohen, and Michael Gold.

651   Hapke, Laura. *Tales of the Working Girl: Wage-Earning Women in American Literature, 1890-1925*. New York: Twayne, 1992.

The focus is on white women in northern urban areas and on how fiction helped shape the debate about the appropriateness of women in the workplace and in unions, because most critical studies of workers in fiction treat only or mainly men, whereas many novels widely read by the middle-class featured working women. Immigrant women workers appear in the novels of James W. Sullivan, Arthur Bullard, Anzia Yezierska, Abraham Cahan, Theodore Dreiser, Edna Ferber, Fannie Hurst, and James Oppenheim.

652   Klein, Marcus. *Foreigners: The Making of American Literature, 1900-1940*. University of Chicago Press, 1981.

Argues that contemporary U.S. literature is a product not only of the New England Puritan tradition but also of the mass immigrations in the twentieth century. Literary "barbarians," or the ethnic writers of the first half of the twentieth century, drove the indigenous American modernists into exile as expatriates in Europe. Michael Gold, Nathanael West, and other immigrant, urban writers tell the new story of an America which shapes the newcomers and is in turn shaped by them.

653   Miller, Wayne C. "Cultural Consciousness in a Multi-Cultural Society: The Uses of Literature." *MELUS* 8:3 (Fall, 1981), 29-41.

Contends that most early white Europeans sought dominance in the new land. Most minority voices seek a space within the society at large while insisting on their own cultural validity.

654   Rideout, Walter B. *The Radical Novel in the United States, 1900-1954*. Cambridge: Harvard University Press, 1956.

A chronologically arranged discussion of fiction having to do with laborers and their involvement with unions, including those that deal with immigrants: Jewish, Abraham Cahan, Elias Tobenkin, Meyer Levin, Michael Gold, and Henry Roth; Irish, Zoe Beckley, James T. Farrell, and Jack Conroy; and Slovak, Thomas Bell.

655 Ruoff, A. LaVonne Brown and Jerry W. Ward, Jr., eds. *Redefining American Literary History.* New York: MLA, 1990.

    Section I, "Redefining the American Literary Canon," contains four essays on the necessity for including minority literatures in classrooms. Section III, "Critical and Historical Perspectives on American Literature," has seven essays, four of which are on Hispanic and Asian literature; and Section IV, "Selected Bibliographies," includes bibliographies on Hispanic, Asian-American, Chicano and Puerto Rican literature in the United States: these appear, where appropriate, in other parts of this bibliography.

656 Salvatori, Mariolina. "Women's Work in Novels of Immigrant Life." *MELUS* 9:4 (Winter, 1982), 39-58.

    Whereas histories of immigration may not pay attention to the woman's part in the history of immigration, that is not true of immigrant novels—such as Norwegian, Rølvaag's *Giants*; Italian, Di Donato's *Christ in Concrete*; Jewish, Yezierska's *Bread Givers*; and Slovak, Bell's *Out of This Furnace*. These books show the importance of women's work in the immigrant experience.

657 Sollors, Werner. *Beyond Ethnicity: Consent and Descent in American Culture.* New York: Oxford University Press, 1986.

    Proposes that American culture, as manifest in texts from Puritan typology to contemporary fiction, attests to ethnic groups that coexist and overlap, because "descent"—heredity—is moderated by "consent"—choice of spouse, career, government, etc. Virtually all Americans can claim an out-group status, and they increasingly seek this romantic, exotic label.

658 ———. "Literature and Ethnicity." *Harvard Encyclopedia of American Ethnic Groups.* Ed. Stephan Thernstrom. Cambridge: Harvard University Press, Belknap, 1980.

    Traces the uses of "ethnicity" throughout the history of American literature and finds that there has been "an amazing amount of cross-cultural, trans-ethnic literature in America." Includes brief discussions of immigrant fiction and contains a bibliography with comments at the end of the article.

659 Sollors, Werner, ed. *The Invention of Ethnicity.* New York: Oxford University Press, 1989.

A collection of essays from several disciplines, though mostly literary criticism and history. Relevant essays are by Mary V. Dearborn on Anzia Yezierska, William Boelhower on immigrant trilogies, and Thomas J. Ferraro on Italian "godfather" fiction.

660 Zyla, Wolodymyr T. and Wendall M. Aycock, eds. *Ethnic Literature Since 1776: The Many Voices of America.* Lubbock: Proceedings of the Comparative Literature Symposium, Texas Tech University, Jan. 1976. IX (1978), 2 vols.

This collection contains essays on a number of writers on the immigrant experience from various ethnic groups. Some of these essays appear in this bibliography under the appropriate groups.

Bibliographies

661 Brieke, Patricia, and Frank J. Sciara. *Selecting Materials for and about Hispanic and East Asian Children and Young People.* New York: Library Professional Publications/Shoe String Press, 1986.

A bibliography of suggested readings, with particular focus on recent immigrants to the United States. Includes brief backgrounds on the history of national or cultural groups within the broader categories.

662 Buttlar, Lois and Lubomyr R. Wynar. *Building Ethnic Collections: An Annotated Guide for School Media Centers and Public Libraries.* Littleton, CO: Libraries Unlimited, 1977.

Contains brief annotated listings for forty-eight ethnic groups, with fiction about the immigrant experience in many of them.

663 Inglehart, Babette F. and Anthony R. Mangione. *The Image of Pluralism in American Literature: An Annotated Bibliography on the Experience of European Ethnic Groups.* New York: Institute of Pluralism and Group Identity of the American Jewish Committee, 1974.

Intended to assist teachers of English and social studies. Includes lists of literary works of eleven ethnic groups, brief plot summaries, and a thematic index: e.g., "Childhood in America," "Cultural Loss or Maintenance," "Education," "Religion," "Work."

664 Miller, Wayne Charles and others. *A Comprehensive Bibliography for the Study of American Minorities*. New York: New York University Press, 1976.

Includes listings for just about every ethnic group in the U.S., with brief annotations on the fiction. The accompanying *Handbook of American Minorities* is a one volume abridgment of the bibliography.

665 Prichard, Nancy S. *A Selected Bibliography of American Ethnic Writing and Supplement*. Champaign: University of Illinois Press, 1969.

Intended for the public schools.

666 Roucek, Joseph S. *The Immigrant in Fiction and Biography*. New York: Bureau for Intercultural Education, 1945.

Two lists alphabetically by ethnic group—one for fiction—with very brief annotations for most of the entries and an indication of suitability for children or young adults.

AUTHOR INDEX

Numbers refer to entries, not pages.

TITLE INDEX

Numbers refer to entries, not pages.

THEME AND GENRE INDEX

Numbers refer to entries, not pages.

Conflicts between generations
2, 4, 11, 50, 51, 58, 59, 65, 67,
69, 79, 83, 87, 100, 104, 105,
107, 130, 142, 147, 148, 150,
152, 168, 175, 180, 182, 187,
216, 230, 235, 250, 252, 259,
263, 269, 276, 283, 299, 302,
303, 305, 306, 311, 312, 318,
319, 330, 337, 355, 357, 374,
380, 382, 383, 384, 396, 397,
431, 445, 465, 501, 510, 520,
522, 538, 540, 579, 599, 604,
629, 630

Conflicts within the immigrant
group 44, 47, 48, 89, 105,
106, 110, 142, 147, 148, 171,
177, 211, 218, 220, 251, 253,
261, 262, 278, 283, 303, 315,
324, 329, 334, 335, 337, 342,
365, 372, 377, 391, 422, 434,
469, 502, 509, 510, 511, 522,
530, 538, 540, 556, 559, 599,
604, 629, 630

Employment
Actor 11, 56, 324
Architect 12
Artist 72, 280, 283, 339, 352,
374, 540, 541
Banker 452
Bartender 11

Business executive 148, 149,
198, 315, 467
Business, owner of large
companies (*see also*
shopowners), breweries 150,
152, carpet 174;
construction 262; food 82;
garbage collection 107;
garment factories 47, 321,
322, 333; import 220, 245,
278; liquor 277; real estate
213; scrap metal 265;
shipping 261, 322;
underworld 278
Camera operator 150
Chicken sexers 295
Clergy 110, 111, 125, 133,
138, 165, 167, 177, 180,
185, 228, 229, 248, 283,
347, 306, 314, 363, 390,
391, 427, 438, 439, 503,
519, 536, 574, 583, 588
Clerical work 209, 218, 339,
353
Construction 106, 133, 257,
262, 528
Domestic labor 65, 92, 153,
203, 204, 221, 315, 358,
384, 422, 424, 504, 606,
611, 612, 613
Dress designer 348, 556

INDEX OF PUBLICATION DATES

Numbers refer to entries, not pages.

372, 394, 425, 519, 530, 536,
543, 552, 557, 575, 583, 591,
596, 598

1970-79 8, 51, 63, 71, 74, 99,
113, 117, 119, 164, 171,172,
175, 181, 205, 206, 207, 244,
245, 247, 261, 282, 297, 299,
300, 306, 311, 320, 323, 336,
348, 373, 374, 375, 376, 386,
387, 388, 395, 428, 429, 430,
431, 433, 436, 438, 443, 451,
454, 460, 466, 468, 469, 521,
525, 529, 534, 537, 539, 540,
544, 545, 568, 574, 600

1980-89 7, 9, 43, 48, 49, 52,
55, 66, 69, 79, 82, 85, 86,
114, 116, 118, 132, 137, 174,
177, 203, 204, 208, 217, 221,
225, 256, 264, 266, 269, 273,
295, 296, 310, 312, 351, 358,
370, 383, 426, 432, 437, 440,
444, 446, 447, 448, 449, 450,
452, 453, 456, 457, 458, 461,
462, 463, 464, 465, 467, 471,
535, 538, 541, 542, 546, 607,
608, 609, 610, 611, 615, 616

1990-94 44, 45, 46, 47, 50,
54, 56, 61, 65, 67, 70, 73, 83,
84, 87, 88, 104, 115, 150,
179, 202, 304, 381, 424, 441,
442, 445, 459, 470, 515, 561,
599, 604, 605, 606, 612

**Anthologies and Secondary
Sources for Ethnic Groups**

1930-39 415, 562

1940-49 159, 291, 525, 572

1950-59 17

1960-69 14, 201, 286, 402,
405, 416, 417, 493, 577

1970-79 16, 18, 22, 23, 25,
27, 97, 121, 162, 238, 289,
313, 400, 401, 403, 404, 406,
409, 411, 414, 421, 473, 475,
477, 478, 480, 481, 492, 495,
532, 563, 565, 576, 580, 582

1980-89 15, 21, 35, 36, 38,
76, 90, 103, 124, 141, 187,
191, 192, 194, 195, 196, 200,
236, 237, 284, 290, 314, 315,
407, 410, 412, 413, 418, 472,
482, 486, 487, 488, 489, 491,
495, 496, 497, 498, 550, 564,
618

**General Anthologies and
Secondary Sources**

1940-49 634, 666

1950-59 654

1960-69 625, 665

1970-79 619, 622, 626, 627,
628, 629, 630, 631, 635, 640,
645, 650, 660, 662, 663, 664

1980-89 621, 623, 636, 641,
642, 643, 644, 646, 647, 648,
652, 653, 656, 657, 659, 661

ABOUT THE AUTHOR

ROBERTA SIMONE (B.S., Northern Illinois State College; M.A., Bowling Green State University; Ohio, Ph.D., University of Illinois, Champaign/Urbana) is Professor of English Language and Literature at Grand Valley State University, Allendale, Michigan. She has served as Chair of the Department and is a member of the honorary fraternity Phi Kappa Phi. She has also taught in the University's Honors Program and in the Liberal Studies Program, for which she developed the course "The Immigrant Experience in the United States." She is the editor of the *Grand Valley Review*, a biannual, interdisciplinary, academic journal. She has published essays and light verse and is presently at work editing a collection of immigrant stories and writing a critical study of themes in immigrant fiction.